CW00517586

AIR FRYING
THE BRITISH WAY

2000-Days Special Recipes for Ninja Dual Zone
Air Fryer, ranging from appetizers and snacks
to main dishes and desserts

NAOMI LANE

Copyright 2023 - Naomi Lane - All rights reserved.

The content contained within this book may not be reproduced, duplicated or transmitted without direct written permission from the author or the publisher.

Under no circumstances will any blame or legal responsibility be held against the publisher, or author, for any damages, reparation, or monetary loss due to the information contained within this book. Either directly or indirectly.

Legal Notice:

This book is copyright protected. This book is only for personal use. You cannot amend, distribute, sell, use, quote or paraphrase any part, or the content within this book, without the consent of the author or publisher.

Disclaimer Notice:

Please note the information contained within this document is for educational and entertainment purposes only. All effort has been executed to present accurate, up to date, and reliable, complete information. No warranties of any kind are declared or implied. Readers acknowledge that the author is not engaging in the rendering of legal, financial, medical or professional advice. The content within this book has been derived from various sources. Please consult a licensed professional before attempting any techniques outlined in this book.

By reading this document, the reader agrees that under no circumstances is the author responsible for any losses, direct or indirect, which are incurred as a result of the use of the information contained within this document, including, but not limited to, errors, omissions, or inaccuracies.

TABLE OF CONTENT

07
SEAFOOD RECIPES............56

08
SNACKS, SANDWICHES AND WRAPS AIR FRYER RECIPES............65

09
PIZZAS & BREAD............73

10
DESURT 83

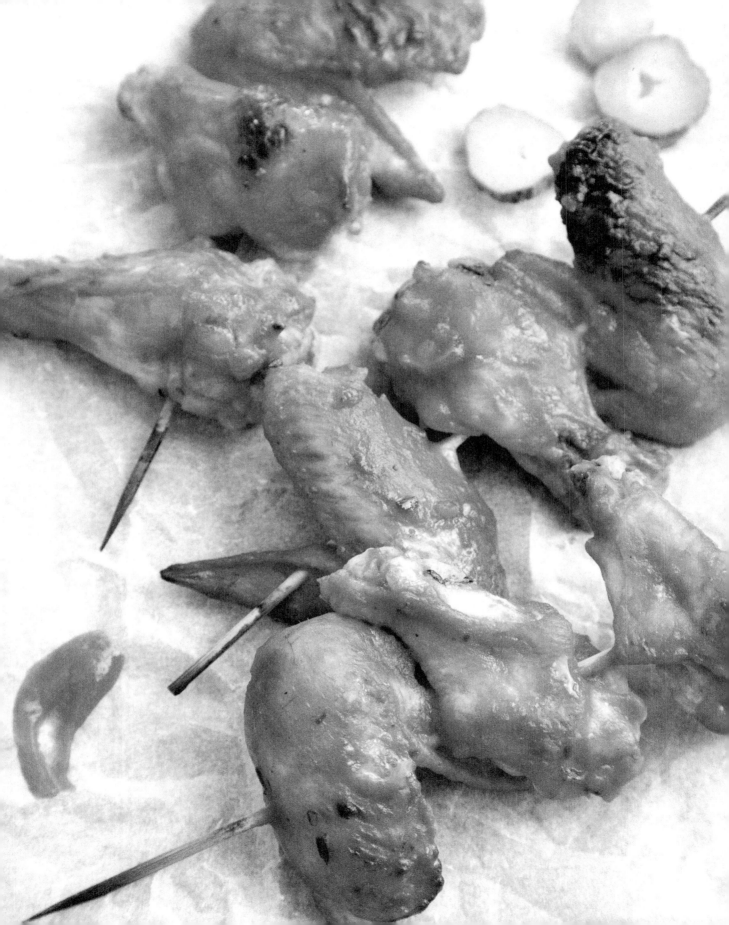

Introduction

The Ninja Dual Zone Air Fryer is not just a simple kitchen appliance, but a game changer in the world of healthy cooking. This innovative appliance allows you to cook meals with less oil, resulting in dishes that are not only delicious, but also healthier for you and your family. The dual-zone technology makes cooking for a large family or entertaining guests a breeze, as you can cook two dishes simultaneously, saving you time and effort in the kitchen.

In this cookbook, we will take you on a culinary journey, exploring the many possibilities of cooking with the Ninja Dual Zone Air Fryer. From appetizers to entrees and even desserts, this cookbook is filled with a wide variety of recipes that are sure to tantalize your taste buds. Each recipe includes detailed instructions and beautiful photographs, making it easy for even the most inexperienced cook to create delicious meals.

In addition to the delicious recipes, this cookbook also includes helpful tips and tricks on how to best use your air fryer. You will learn about the different cooking functions and how to adjust the temperature and time settings to achieve the perfect results every time. We will also cover the different types of food that can be cooked in an air fryer, including vegetables, meats, and even frozen foods.

So, whether you're looking to eat healthier, save time in the kitchen, or just want to try something new, the Ninja Dual Zone Air Fryer Cookbook is the perfect resource for you. With its easy-to-follow recipes and helpful tips, this cookbook will help you create delicious and healthy meals that you and your family will love. So, let's start cooking and discover the many benefits of the Ninja Dual Zone Air Fryer!

Chapter 1: Important Safeguards

A. Safety Precautions

It is important to always use oven mitts or tongs to handle hot food or the air fryer basket. Do not touch the heating elements or interior surfaces of the air fryer while in use, as they can become very hot. Keep the air fryer away from flammable materials, such as curtains or paper towels, to prevent fire. It is also important to keep the air fryer away from water and other liquids to prevent electrical shock. The air fryer should only be used indoors and should never be used outdoors.

B. Electrical Requirements

The air fryer must be connected to a properly grounded electrical outlet, and should only be used with the electrical voltage and frequency specified on the rating label. It is not recommended to use an extension cord or adapter with the air fryer.

C. Grounding Instructions

The air fryer must be grounded to reduce the risk of electrical shock in the event of an electrical short circuit. Grounding provides a path of least resistance for electric current, making it an important safety feature. If the air fryer is not properly grounded, it may cause an electrical shock or fire.

Chapter 2: Operating Buttons

A. Overview of the Control Panel

The control panel of the Ninja Foodi Dual-Zone Air Fryer is designed with the user in mind. It includes several buttons and displays that allow you to easily adjust the temperature and time settings, as well as select the cooking function that is best suited for each dish.

The temperature and time settings can be adjusted using the + and - buttons. The temperature can be adjusted in increments of 2.8°C, and the time can be adjusted in increments of 1 minute. The display shows the current temperature and time settings, as well as a timer that counts down the cooking time.

The cooking function can be selected using the function buttons, which include air fry, bake, and broil. The air fry function uses hot air to cook food, resulting in crispy and delicious dishes without the need for unhealthy oils. The bake function is ideal for cooking casseroles, cakes, and other baked goods. The broil function is perfect for cooking meats, vegetables, and other dishes that require a crispy exterior.

In addition to these buttons, the control panel may also include a start/stop button, a power button, and a timer button. The start/stop button allows you to start and pause the cooking process, while the power button turns the air fryer on and off. The timer button can be used to set a timer for the cooking process.

With its clear and easy-to-use controls, the Ninja Foodi Dual-Zone Air Fryer makes it simple to cook a wide variety of meals with confidence. Whether you're cooking a delicate fish fillet or a hearty roast, you can easily adjust the temperature, time, and cooking function to achieve the perfect results every time.

B. Understanding the Cooking Functions

The Ninja Foodi Dual-Zone Air Fryer is equipped with several cooking functions that allow you to cook a wide variety of meals to perfection. The three main cooking functions are air fry, bake, and broil.

The air fry function uses hot air to cook food, resulting in crispy and delicious dishes without the need for unhealthy oils. This function is perfect for cooking a wide range of foods, including chicken, fish, French fries, and more. The hot air circulates around the food, cooking it evenly and thoroughly, and the food is crisp and golden on the outside, tender and juicy on the inside.

The bake function allows you to cook casseroles, cakes, and other baked goods. This function uses gentle heat to cook the food slowly and evenly, resulting in perfectly baked dishes every time. Whether you're baking a cake, a casserole, or a loaf of bread, the bake function ensures that your food will come out perfectly every time.

The broil function is ideal for cooking meats, vegetables, and other dishes that require a crispy exterior. This function uses high heat to cook the food quickly and thoroughly, resulting in perfectly broiled dishes every time. Whether you're cooking steak, chicken, or vegetables, the broil function ensures that your food will come out perfectly crisp and delicious.

With these cooking functions, you can easily create a wide range of meals to suit your tastes and dietary needs. Whether you're cooking a quick and easy weeknight dinner or a special occasion meal, the Ninja Foodi Dual-Zone Air Fryer has the versatility and performance you need to cook with confidence.

C. Adjusting the Temperature and Time Settings

The temperature and time settings on the Ninja Foodi Dual-Zone Air Fryer can be adjusted to suit the specific needs of each dish. This allows you to cook a wide variety of meals to perfection, ensuring that each dish is cooked evenly and to the desired doneness.

The temperature can be adjusted in increments of 2.8°C, allowing you to fine-tune the cooking temperature to suit the needs of each dish. For example, when cooking chicken, you may want to use a higher temperature to ensure that the chicken is cooked through, while when cooking a delicate fish fillet, you may want to use a lower temperature to prevent the fish from becoming too dry.

The time can be adjusted in increments of 1 minute, allowing you to set the cooking time for each dish. The timer counts down the cooking time, so you can easily monitor the progress of your meal. When the cooking time is up, the air fryer will automatically shut off, alerting you that your meal is ready.

By adjusting the temperature and time settings, you can cook a wide variety of meals with confidence, ensuring that each dish is cooked perfectly every time. Whether you're cooking a quick and easy weeknight dinner or a special occasion meal, the Ninja Foodi Dual-Zone Air

Fryer makes it easy to achieve the perfect results every time.

Chapter 3: Benefits of the Ninja Foodi Dual-Zone Air Fryer

A. Healthy Cooking

One of the main benefits of the Ninja Foodi Dual-Zone Air Fryer is its ability to cook food in a healthy and delicious way. With its air fry function, you can cook a wide range of foods, including chicken, fish, French fries, and more, without the need for unhealthy oils. The hot air circulates around the food, cooking it evenly and thoroughly, and the food is crisp and golden on the outside, tender and juicy on the inside. This means you can enjoy your favorite foods without sacrificing taste or health.

B. Dual-Zone Cooking

Another benefit of the Ninja Foodi Dual-Zone Air Fryer is its dual-zone cooking capability. This means that you can cook two different dishes at the same time, each in its own basket. This is perfect for families or for those who like to cook multiple dishes for meal prep. The dual-zone cooking capability also makes it easy to cook a complete meal, with each dish being cooked to perfection in its own basket. This saves you time and effort, as you can cook multiple dishes at once, without having to wait for one dish to finish cooking before starting the next.

C. Versatile Cooking

The Ninja Foodi Dual-Zone Air Fryer is also incredibly versatile, allowing you to cook a wide range of dishes, including baked goods, broiled meats, and more. With its bake and broil functions, you can cook casseroles, cakes, and other baked goods, as well as broiled meats, vegetables, and more. The versatility of the air fryer makes it an ideal appliance for creating delicious and healthy meals for you and your family. Whether you're cooking a quick and easy weeknight dinner or a special occasion meal, the Ninja Foodi Dual-Zone Air Fryer has the versatility and performance you need to cook with confidence.

D. Easy to Clean

The Ninja Foodi Dual-Zone Air Fryer is also easy to clean. The air fryer baskets and drip tray are dishwasher safe, making cleaning up a breeze. The air fryer itself can also be easily wiped clean with a damp cloth. With its easy-to-clean design, the Ninja Foodi Dual-Zone Air Fryer is the perfect appliance for busy families or for those who want to spend less time cleaning up after cooking.

E. Energy Efficient

In addition to its many benefits, the Ninja Foodi Dual-Zone Air Fryer is also energy efficient. This means that it uses less energy than traditional cooking methods, such as ovens and stovetops, making it an eco-friendly choice for your home. By using less energy, you can save money on your energy bills and reduce your carbon footprint.

F. Convenient and Portable

The Ninja Foodi Dual-Zone Air Fryer is also convenient and portable. Its compact design makes it easy to store in your kitchen, and its lightweight and easy-to-carry design makes it easy to take with you on the go. Whether you're cooking at home or on the road, the Ninja Foodi Dual-Zone Air Fryer is the perfect appliance for healthy and convenient cooking.

Chapter 4: Before First Use

Before using your Ninja Foodi Dual-Zone Air Fryer for the first time, it is important to take a few steps to ensure that it is ready to use and that you are familiar with its functions.

First, inspect the air fryer for any damage that may have occurred during shipping. If there is any damage, do not use the air fryer and contact the manufacturer for assistance. Next, remove all packaging materials, including any protective plastic wrap or foam, and dispose of them properly. Keep all documentation, including the owner's manual and the warranty card, for future reference.

It is also important to clean the air fryer before first use. This will ensure that any residue from the manufacturing process is removed and that your air fryer is ready to use. To clean the air fryer, simply wipe it down with a damp cloth and dry it thoroughly.

Familiarizing yourself with the operating buttons and cooking functions is also crucial before using your air fryer for the first time. The control panel on the air fryer includes buttons for adjusting the temperature and time, as well as buttons for selecting the cooking function. The owner's manual provides detailed information on the operating buttons and cooking functions, as well as helpful tips for using your air fryer.

Additionally, it is important to understand the benefits of the Ninja Foodi Dual-Zone Air Fryer. The air fryer is designed to cook food in a healthy and delicious way, with its air fry function allowing you to cook a wide range of foods without the need for unhealthy oils. The air fryer also features dual-zone cooking, allowing you to cook two different dishes at the same time, each in its own basket. Additionally, the air fryer is incredibly versatile, allowing you to cook a wide range of dishes, including baked goods, broiled meats, and more.

By following these steps and familiarizing yourself with the functions of the air fryer, you can ensure that your air fryer is ready to use and that you are able to cook delicious and healthy meals with confidence. Whether you're cooking a quick and easy weeknight dinner or a special occasion meal, the Ninja Foodi Dual-Zone Air Fryer is the perfect appliance for healthy and convenient cooking.

Chapter 5: Cleaning Your Ninja Foodi Dual-Zone Air Fryer

It is important to clean your Ninja Foodi Dual-Zone Air Fryer after each use to ensure that it continues to function properly and to maintain its appearance. The air fryer baskets and drip tray are dishwasher safe, making cleaning up a breeze. The air fryer itself can also be easily wiped clean with a damp cloth.

To clean the air fryer baskets and drip tray, simply place them in the dishwasher and run a normal cycle. If you prefer to wash them by hand, use warm soapy water and a soft sponge to gently clean them, being careful not to scratch the surface. Rinse the baskets and tray thoroughly and dry them completely before using them again.

To clean the air fryer itself, simply wipe it down with a damp cloth and dry it thoroughly. Do not use harsh chemicals or abrasive cleaners, as they can damage the surface of the air fryer. If there are any tough stains or spots, you can use a mild soap and water solution to clean them.

By cleaning your Ninja Foodi Dual-Zone Air Fryer after each use, you can ensure that it continues to function properly and that it maintains its appearance for years to come. With its easy-to-clean design, the Ninja Foodi Dual-Zone Air Fryer is the perfect appliance for busy families or for those who want to spend less time cleaning up after cooking.

Chapter 6: Helpful Tips

Preheat the Air Fryer: Preheating the air fryer before cooking is an important step in ensuring that your food is cooked evenly and thoroughly. To preheat the air fryer, simply set the temperature and time for your desired cooking function and allow the air fryer to preheat for a few minutes before adding your food.

Shake the Baskets: Shaking the baskets occasionally during cooking can help to ensure that the food is cooked evenly. This is especially important when cooking foods like French fries or chicken wings, which can become unevenly cooked if left stationary in the basket. To shake the baskets, simply pause the cooking process and gently shake the baskets to redistribute the food.

Consider Cooking Time and Temperature: When cooking multiple dishes at the same time, it is important to consider the cooking time and temperature for each dish. For example, if you are cooking a dish that requires a higher temperature in one basket and a dish that requires a lower temperature in the other basket, you may need to stagger the cooking time so that both dishes are finished cooking at the same time.

Keep the Air Fryer Clean: Keeping the air fryer clean and free of any debris that may accumulate during cooking is important for proper functioning and appearance. To clean the air fryer, simply wipe it down with a damp cloth and dry it thoroughly. The air fryer baskets and drip tray are dishwasher safe, making cleaning up a breeze.

Experiment with Different Cooking Functions: The Ninja Foodi Dual-Zone Air Fryer offers a variety of cooking functions, including air fry, bake, broil, and more. Experiment with these different functions to see which works best for your favorite dishes.

Use the Right Accessories: The air fryer comes with a range of accessories, including air fry baskets and drip trays. Be sure to use the right accessories for each dish to ensure that it cooks evenly and to prevent any messes.

Use a Meat Thermometer: To ensure that your food is cooked to the right temperature, use a meat thermometer to check the internal temperature of your dishes. This is especially important when cooking meat, poultry, and fish, as undercooked meat can pose a health risk.

Cook in Batches: If you're cooking for a large family or entertaining guests, you may need to cook in batches to ensure that all of the food is cooked evenly and to the desired temperature.

Try New Recipes: The Ninja Foodi Dual-Zone Air Fryer opens up a world of cooking possibilities. Try new recipes, experiment with different ingredients, and have fun cooking with this versatile appliance.

Cook Foods in a Single Layer: For best results, try to cook foods in a single layer in the air fryer baskets. This will help to ensure even cooking and prevent overcrowding, which can result in uneven cooking.

Don't Overcrowd the Baskets: Overcrowding the air fryer baskets can result in uneven cooking and can also reduce the air flow, making it more difficult for the air fryer to cook the food properly. To avoid overcrowding, make sure that there is enough space between the pieces of food in the baskets.

Stir or Flip Foods Regularly: Stirring or flipping foods regularly during cooking can help to ensure even cooking and prevent burning. This is especially important when cooking foods like vegetables, which can become unevenly cooked if left stationary in the basket.

Adjust Cooking Time and Temperature as Needed: Cooking time and temperature can vary depending on the type and size of the food being cooked, as well as the desired level of doneness. Be prepared to adjust the cooking time and temperature as needed to ensure that the food is cooked to your liking.

Use Non-Stick Cooking Spray: To prevent foods from sticking to the air fryer baskets, consider using a non-stick cooking spray before cooking. This will also help to make cleaning up easier.

Chapter 7: Replacement Parts

From time to time, it may be necessary to replace certain parts of your Ninja Foodi Dual-Zone Air Fryer. This could be due to normal wear and tear, accidental damage, or other factors. If you need to replace a part of your air fryer, it is important to use only genuine Ninja Foodi replacement parts to ensure that your air fryer continues to function properly and to maintain its warranty.

Common replacement parts for the Ninja Foodi Dual-Zone Air Fryer include the air fry baskets, drip tray, and heating element. These parts can be easily replaced and are readily available from the manufacturer or from authorized dealers.

To replace a part of your air fryer, simply follow the instructions provided in the owner's manual or on the manufacturer's website. If you need assistance or have any questions, contact the manufacturer or an authorized dealer for help.

By using only genuine Ninja Foodi replacement parts, you can ensure that your air fryer continues to function properly and that your investment is protected. Whether you're replacing a worn-out part or upgrading your air fryer, the right replacement parts can help to keep your air fryer in top condition for years to come.

Chapter 8: Troubleshooting

The Ninja Foodi Dual-Zone Air Fryer is a reliable and durable appliance, but from time to time, you may encounter issues that need to be addressed. In this chapter, we will discuss some of the most common problems that you may encounter and how to resolve them.

Not Turning On: If your air fryer is not turning on, the first step is to check the power source. Make sure that the air fryer is properly plugged in and that the outlet is functioning. If the problem persists, check the power cord for any visible damage and replace it if necessary. If the power cord is in good condition, check the heating element for any visible damage and replace it if necessary.

Not Heating Up: If your air fryer is not heating up, check the temperature settings to make sure that they are set correctly. If the temperature settings are correct, check the heating element for any visible damage and replace it if necessary. If the heating element is in good condition, check the power cord and outlet for any issues.

Food Not Cooking Evenly: If your food is not cooking evenly, the first step is to check the baskets to make sure that they are not overcrowded. The air fryer works best when the food is arranged in a single layer in the baskets. If the baskets are not overcrowded, consider shaking the baskets occasionally during cooking to redistribute the food.

Strange Noises: If your air fryer is making strange noises, check to make sure that the baskets are properly aligned and that there are no loose parts. If the baskets are properly aligned and there are no loose parts, check the fan blade and motor for any visible damage and replace them if necessary.

Other Issues: If you encounter any other issues with your air fryer, refer to the owner's manual or contact the manufacturer or an authorized dealer for assistance. They can provide you with guidance on how to resolve the issue and get your air fryer back up and running as quickly as possible.

01 | **Breakfast**
Recipes

1. Easy Bread Sticks for Breakfast

 Prep: 15 Mi nutes | **Cook Time:** 8 Minutes | **Makes:** 2 Servings

INGREDIENTS

- 5 thick Texas toast slice
- 3 organic eggs, lightly beaten
- ½ cup almond milk
- Two drops vanilla extract
- Few pinches of cinnamon powder
- 2 pinches of ground cardamom powder

DIRECTIONS

- The first step is to preheat the air fryer at 400 degrees F (204 degrees) for 3 minutes.
- Take about 5 bread slices and cut the slices into thirds to make sticks.
- Take an air fryer basket and line it with parchment paper that fits inside it easily.
- Take a large mixing bowl and pour almond milk in it, then add vanilla extract, cinnamon, and cardamom powder.
- Stir it well and next whisk egg in a bowl and add it to the milk mixture, whisk eggs well with milk.
- Now dip each bread stick in the egg wash and then single layer it on the basket of the air fryer according to capacity.
- The bread needed to be cooked in batches.
- Cook it for 8 minutes at 375 degrees F (190 degrees C).
- Flip after 4 minutes of cooking.
- Once it's done, serve as a delicious breakfast.

NUTRITION FACTS

Servings	:	2

Amount per serving
Calories 488

% Daily Value*

Total Fat	23. 4g	30%
Total Carbohydrate	51.6g	19%
Protein	17.2g	

2. Toad-In-The-Hole

 Prep: 15 Minutes | **Cook Time:** 20 Minutes | **Makes:** 4 Servings

INGREDIENTS

- 1 large sheet frozen puff pastry, thawed
- 4 tablespoons Parmesan cheese, shredded
- 4 tablespoons diced spam
- 4 eggs, organic
- 4 tablespoons heavy cream

DIRECTIONS

- The first step is to preheat the air fryer to 400 degrees F (204 degrees C).
- Take out the pastry sheet and unfold it on a clean kitchen counter.
- Cut the sheet into four equal squares.
- Take the sheet and add them to the air fryer basket and cook for 5 minutes.
- Once puffed remove from the air fryer and set aside for further use.
- Press the cooked squares with a spoon so that they created an indentation.

- Then start layering each of the squares with 1 tablespoon of cheese and 1 tablespoon of spam.
- Pour one egg on top of each square.
- Put it back in the basket and cook for 5-7 minutes.
- Repeat these entire steps with the remaining squares.
- Once it's done serve with a garnish of cream.

NUTRITION FACTS

Servings: 4

Amount per serving
Calories 589

% Daily Value*
Total Fat	42.3g	54%
Total Carbohydrate	30.6g	11%
Protein	22.9g	

3. Simple Breakfast Frittata

 Prep: 15 Minutes | **Cook Time:** 18 Minutes | **Makes:** 4 Servings

INGREDIENTS

- 1/3 pound sausage, cooked and crumbled
- 6 small eggs, lightly beaten
- ½ cup cheddar cheese, shredded
- 4 tablespoons green bell pepper, chopped
- ½ green onion, chopped
- Pinch of salt
- Pinch of black pepper
- Oil spray, for greasing

DIRECTIONS

- The first step is to preheat the air fryer at 360 degrees F (182 degrees C).
- Next, take a large bowl and add sausage, eggs, cheese, green bell pepper, onions, salt, and black pepper.
- Mix it very well.
- Oil greased a cake pan that fits inside the air fryer basket.
- Pour the prepared mixture into the cake pan.
- Cook it in the air fryer for 18 to 20 minutes.
- Once done, serve and enjoy.

NUTRITION FACTS

Servings: 4

Amount per serving
Calories 304

% Daily Value*
Total Fat	21.4g	27%
Total Carbohydrate	9.8g	4%
Protein	19.1g	

4. Breakfast Potato Hash

 Prep: 15 Minutes | **Cook Time:** 20 Minutes | **Makes:** 3 Servings

INGREDIENTS

- 4 Potatoes, peeled and chopped
- 1 teaspoon butter, melted
- ½ tablespoon of olive oil
- 1 small green onion, chopped
- 1 Green Pepper, chopped
- ¼ teaspoon Savory
- 1/3 teaspoon thyme
- ¼ teaspoon of red chili flakes
- Salt and black pepper, to taste
- 3-6 eggs

DIRECTIONS

- Preheat the air fryer at 390 degrees F (198 degrees C) for 5 minutes.
- Take a cooking pan and melt butter in it.
- Then add olive oil and cook for 30 seconds.
- Now cook onions in it for 1 minute and add potatoes and green peppers.
- Cook it for 5 minutes and season it with savory, thyme, salt, red chili flakes, and black pepper.
- Transfer it to the air fryer basket and air fry for 18 minutes.
- Meanwhile, oil sprays a cooking pan and cooks eggs according to personal preference.
- Once the potato hash is ready, serve it with eggs on top.
- Enjoy.

NUTRITION FACTS

Servings: 3

Amount per serving
Calories 458

% Daily Value*
Total Fat	8.7g	11%
Total Carbohydrate	80.6g	29%
Protein	15.1g	

5. Breakfast Hard Boiled Eggs with Stuffing:

- 4 large organic eggs
- Handful of baby spinach
- 4 tablespoons of tomato paste
- 4 tablespoons of mayonnaise
- Salt and black pepper, to taste
- 1 lemon, juice only
- Water, for boiling

DIRECTIONS:

- Preheat the air fryer to 200°C (392°F) for 5 minutes.
- Boil water in a large cooking pot.
- Thaw the spinach in the water and set it aside.
- Chop the spinach with a knife.
- Place the eggs in the air fryer basket and cook for 12-15 minutes.
- Remove the eggs and let them cool.
- Peel the eggs and cut them in half lengthwise.
- Scoop out the yolks and place them in a bowl.
- Add the chopped spinach, mayonnaise, and chopped tomato paste to the bowl.
- Stir to combine and season with salt, black pepper, and lemon juice.
- Fill each egg white with the mixture.
- Serve and enjoy.

6. Peanut Butter Filled Holes:

- 1 can of biscuits
- 250g peanut butter, chunky
- 50g butter, salted
- Oil spray, for greasing

DIRECTIONS:

- Preheat the air fryer to 200°C (392°F) for 5 minutes.
- Grease the air fryer basket with oil spray.
- Cut the biscuits into 20 small pieces.
- Flatten the pieces on a flat surface with a rolling pin.
- Place a tablespoon of peanut butter in the center of each piece and wrap the dough around it to seal the edges.
- Brush the doughnuts with butter and place them in the air fryer basket.
- Cook in batches for 12 minutes, rotating the holes halfway through.
- Serve and enjoy.

7. Air Fryer English Style Breakfast:

- 4 breakfast sausages
- 4 bacon strips, unsmoked
- 4 organic eggs
- 450g baked beans
- 4 slices of whole wheat bread
- A few slices of smoked tomatoes
- Oil spray, for greasing

DIRECTIONS:

- Preheat the air fryer to 162°C (325°F) for 5 minutes.
- Place the bacon strips and sausages in the oil-greased air fryer basket and cook for 5 minutes.
- Remove the sausage and bacon and set them aside.
- Grease two ramekins with oil spray.
- Pour the baked beans into the ramekins and cook in the air fryer basket for 8 minutes.
- Fry the eggs in a frying pan.
- Arrange the cooked bacon, sausages, baked beans, fried eggs, and smoked tomato slices on a plate. Serve and enjoy.

8. Tapioca Cheesy Bread:

Prep Time: 12 Minutes	Cook Time: 18 Minutes	Serves: 4

INGREDIENTS:

- 173g Tapioca flour
- 2 teaspoons baking powder
- 173g cheddar cheese
- 173g Swiss cheese
- 2 large organic eggs, whisked
- 60ml heavy cream

INSTRUCTIONS:

- In a large bowl, mix 140g of tapioca flour, baking powder, cheddar cheese, Swiss cheese, whisked eggs, and heavy cream.
- Mix to form dough.
- Knead the dough onto a flat surface using the remaining 33g of tapioca flour.
- Let the dough sit for 30 minutes.
- Transfer the dough to a loaf pan lined with parchment paper.
- Place the loaf pan inside the air fryer and cook for 15-18 minutes at 204°C.
- Remove from the air fryer, let it cool before slicing.

NUTRITION INFORMATION (PER SERVING):

Calories:	554
Fat:	30.7g (39% of daily value)
Carbohydrates:	43.1g (16% of daily value)
Protein:	25.3g

9. Potatoes for Breakfast:

 Prep Time: 15 Minutes | **Cook Time:** 40 Minutes | **Serves:** 4

INGREDIENTS:

- 450g large russet potatoes, scrubbed and diced
- 1 medium onion, diced
- 2 green peppers, diced
- 30ml olive oil
- Salt, to taste
- 2 teaspoons onion powder
- 1 teaspoon garlic powder
- 1/2 teaspoon paprika
- Water, as needed

INSTRUCTIONS:

- Preheat the air fryer to 200°C.
- Fill a bowl with water and soak the potatoes for 20 minutes.
- In a mixing bowl, add the remaining ingredients, except for the potatoes.
- Grease the air fryer basket with oil spray.
- Drain the potatoes and pat dry with a paper towel.
- Coat the potatoes in the bowl with the remaining ingredients.
- Add the coated potatoes to the air fryer basket.
- Bake in the air fryer for 40 minutes at 200°C. Remember to shake the basket during cooking.
- Once done, serve.
- Nutrition Information (Per serving):
Calories: 281
- Fat: 7.5g (10% of daily value)
- Carbohydrates: 50.4g (18% of daily value)
Protein: 5.7g

10. Air Fryer Polenta Bites:

 Prep Time: 15 Minutes | **Cook Time:** 16 Minutes | **Serves:** 4

INGREDIENTS:

- 1 packet of polenta
- 120g potato starch
- Oil spray, for greasing

Topping Ingredients:

- Maple syrup, as needed

INSTRUCTIONS:

- Preheat the air fryer to 198°C.
- Dust the polenta balls with potato starch and place on an oil sprayed cookie sheet.
- Grease the polenta balls with oil spray.
- Place the cookie sheet inside the air fryer basket.
- Cook for 8 minutes.
- Flip the polenta balls and cook for another 8 minutes.
- Serve with topping.

 NUTRITION INFORMATION (PER SERVING):

Calories:	429
Fat:	0.4g (1% of daily value)
Carbohydrates:	101.5g (37% of daily value)
Protein:	1.9g

11. Eggs and Ham Muffins

 Prep: 20 Minutes | **Cook Time:** 15 Minutes | **Serves:** 4

INGREDIENTS:

- 170g Ham, sliced into pieces
- A handful of baby spinach
- 6 organic eggs
- 6 tablespoons full-fat milk
- 1 tablespoon olive oil
- Salt and black pepper, to taste
- Oil spray for greasing

INSTRUCTIONS:

- Preheat the air fryer to 190°C.
- Grease about 6 ramekins with oil spray.
- Heat the oil in a frying pan and stir-fry the baby spinach for 1 minute.
- Divide the ham evenly among the ramekins.
- In a mixing bowl, whisk the eggs together with the milk and olive oil.
- Add the cooked spinach to the egg mixture and mix well.
- Pour the egg mixture evenly into the ramekins.
- Season with salt and black pepper.
- Place the ramekins in the air fryer basket and cook for 15 minutes.
- Serve.

NUTRITION INFORMATION:

Servings: 4

Per serving:
Calories: 208
Fat: 14.4g (18% of daily value)
Carbohydrates: 3.6g (1% of daily value)
Protein: 16.3g

12. Eggs in a Bowl of Bread

 Prep: 15 Minutes **Cook Time:** 22 Minutes **Serves:** 3

INGREDIENTS:

- 3 dinner rolls
- 3 large organic eggs
- 2 tablespoons parsley
- Salt and black pepper, to taste
- 1 tablespoon chopped chives
- 100g grated Parmesan cheese

INSTRUCTIONS:

- Cut the tops off of three dinner rolls and remove some of the bread from the center to create a cavity large enough to hold an egg.
- Arrange the rolls in an oiled air fryer basket.
- Crack one egg into each cavity.
- Sprinkle parsley, salt, black pepper, chives, and Parmesan cheese on top of the eggs.
- Place the air fryer basket inside the air fryer and cook at 176°C for 18-22 minutes.
- Serve warm.

NUTRITION INFORMATION:

Servings: 3

Per serving:
Calories: 519
Fat: 22.6g (29% of daily value)
Carbohydrates: 47.4g (17% of daily value)
Protein: 33.7g

13. Breakfast Muffin Sandwich

 Prep: 15 Minutes **Cook Time:** 12 Minutes **Serves:** 2

INGREDIENTS:

- 2 organic eggs
- 4 rashers of bacon
- 2 English muffins

INSTRUCTIONS:

- Crack one egg into each of two heat-resistant soufflé cups.
- Place the cups in the air fryer basket and cook for 6 minutes at 204°C.
- Remove the cups from the air fryer and oil spray the basket.
- Add the bacon and English muffins, misted with oil spray, to the basket and cook for 6 minutes.
- Split the muffins in half and assemble the sandwich with the eggs and bacon.
- Serve.

NUTRITION INFORMATION:

Servings: 2

Per serving:
Calories: 332
Fat: 17.3g (22% of daily value)
Carbohydrates: 25.5g (9% of daily value)
Vitamin D: 15mcg

14. Chipolatas with Eggs

 Prep: 15 Minutes **Cook Time:** 16 Minutes **Serves:** 4

INGREDIENTS:

- 6 chestnut mushrooms
- 6 halved cherry tomatoes
- 2 cloves of crushed garlic
- 4 smoked bacon rashers
- 4 chipolatas
- 4 organic eggs
- Salt and black pepper, to taste
- Oil spray for greasing

INSTRUCTIONS:

- Preheat the air fryer to 204°C for 5 minutes.
- Grease a round tin that fits inside the air fryer basket with oil spray.
- In a mixing bowl, combine the tomatoes, salt, black pepper, garlic, and mushrooms and mist with oil spray.
- Add the bacon and chipolatas to the tin and place the tin in the air fryer basket.
- Cook for 12 minutes in the air fryer.

- Meanwhile, cook the eggs in a non-stick frying pan.
- Serve the tin ingredients with the eggs as a delicious breakfast.

 NUTRITION INFORMATION:

Servings:	4

Per serving:
Calories: 275
- Fat: 17.6g (23% of daily value)
- Carbohydrates: 10.4g (4% of daily value)
Protein: 19.9g

15. Breakfast Omelet

Prep: 15 Minutes	**Cook Time:** 16 Minutes	**Serves:** 4

INGREDIENTS:

- 4 eggs
- 25g butter
- 60ml full-fat milk
- 125g grated cheese
- Salt and black pepper, to taste
- 1 small onion, chopped
- Oil spray for greasing

INSTRUCTIONS:

- Preheat the air fryer to 176°C for 5 minutes.
- In a medium bowl, whisk the eggs with the butter and milk.
- Add the grated cheese and mix well.
- Season with salt and black pepper.
- Stir in the chopped onion.
- Pour the omelet mixture into a greased cake pan.
- Place the pan in the air fryer basket and cook for 8-10 minutes.
- Serve hot.

 NUTRITION INFORMATION:

Servings:	4

Per serving:
Calories: 163
Fat: 12.6g (16% of daily value)
Carbohydrates: 2.9g (1% of daily value)
Protein: 9.8g

16. Cheesy Eggs in a Hole

Prep: 10 Minutes	**Cook Time:** 10 Minutes	**Serves:** 2

INGREDIENTS:

- 2 slices of bread
- Salt and black pepper, to taste
- 2 eggs
- Oil spray for greasing
- 2 slices of cheddar cheese

INSTRUCTIONS:

- Cut a hole in the center of each slice of bread with a small round cutter.
- Grease the air fryer basket with oil spray or line it with parchment paper.
- Arrange the bread slices in the basket.
- Crack one egg into each hole and season with salt and black pepper.
- Cook in the air fryer at 176°C for 6-8 minutes.
- Remove the basket from the air fryer and top each slice of bread with a slice of cheese.
- Return the basket to the air fryer and cook for 2 more minutes, until the cheese has melted.
- Serve.

 NUTRITION INFORMATION:

Servings:	2

Per serving:
Calories: 202
Fat: 14.2g (18% of daily value)
Carbohydrates: 5.3g (2% of daily value)
Protein: 13.2g

17. Breakfast Tortilla Wraps

Prep: 15 Minutes	**Cook Time:** 13 Minutes	**Serves:** 4

INGREDIENTS:

- 4 cooked and sliced chicken breasts (100g each)
- 8 eggs, whisked
- 1/2 avocado, chopped
- 250g grated mozzarella cheese
- Salt and black pepper, to taste
- 4 tortilla wraps

INSTRUCTIONS:

- Preheat the air fryer to 176°C for 5 minutes.
- In a medium bowl, whisk the eggs with salt and black pepper.

- Grease a shallow tin with oil spray and pour the egg mixture into the tin.
- Place the tin in the air fryer basket and cook for 8 minutes.
- Once the eggs are done, divide the egg mixture, chicken, cheese, and avocado among the tortilla wraps.
- Place the tortilla wraps on an air fryer basket lined with aluminum foil and cook for 5 minutes.
- Serve.

 NUTRITION INFORMATION:

Servings: 4

Per serving:
Calories: 511
Fat: 21.9g (28% of daily value)
Carbohydrates: 34.1g (12% of daily value)
Protein: 42.8g

18. Three Berries Muffins

 Prep: 20 Minutes | **Cook Time:** 24 Minutes | **Serves:** 4

INGREDIENTS:

- 175g whole wheat flour
- 185g oatmeal
- 100g brown sugar
- 2 tablespoons baking powder
- 125g fresh blueberries
- 85g fresh strawberries
- 60g fresh raspberries
- 1/3 teaspoon cinnamon
- A pinch of sea salt
- 250ml coconut milk
- 60g melted butter
- 2 eggs, whisked

INSTRUCTIONS:

- Preheat the air fryer to 176ºC for 5 minutes.
- In a large bowl, mix the flour, oatmeal, brown sugar, baking powder, cinnamon, and sea salt.
- In a separate bowl, whisk the eggs and add the coconut milk.
- Add the melted butter to the egg mixture and mix well.
- Mix the contents of both bowls and fold in the berries.
- Divide the batter evenly among 8 lined muffin cups in ramekins.
- Place the cups in batches in the air fryer basket and cook for 12 minutes per batch.
- Serve.

 NUTRITION INFORMATION:

Servings: 4

Per serving:
Calories: 449
Fat: 29.3g (38% of daily value)
Carbohydrates: 45.1g (16% of daily value)
Protein: 7.6g

19. Egg in an Avocado

 Prep Time: 10 Minutes | **Cook Time:** 5 Minutes | **Serves:** 2

INGREDIENTS:

- 1 large avocado, pitted and cut in half
- Oil spray for greasing
- 2 small organic eggs
- 1/3 teaspoon paprika powder
- Salt and freshly ground black pepper to taste
- 1 teaspoon chopped chives

INSTRUCTIONS:

- Preheat the air fryer to 190ºC (375ºF) for 5 minutes.
- Cut the avocado in half and remove the seed and some of the flesh to create a cavity for the egg.
- Crack one egg into each cavity of the avocado.
- Sprinkle the salt, paprika, and black pepper on top of the eggs.
- Lightly spray the air fryer basket with oil spray and place the avocado halves in the basket.
- Place the basket in the air fryer and cook for 5 minutes.
- Serve hot, garnished with chopped chives.
- Nutrition Information (per serving):
Calories: 359 | Total Fat: 30.6g (39%) | Total Carbohydrates: 9.9g   (4%) | Protein: 6

20. Walnut and Cornmeal Muffins

 Prep Time: 15 Minutes | **Cook Time:** 32 Minutes | **Serves:** 4

INGREDIENTS:

- 50g cornmeal
- 50g plain flour
- 1 teaspoon baking powder

- Pinch of salt
- 50g white sugar
- 1 teaspoon grated orange zest
- 60ml orange juice
- 30g butter, melted
- 2 small eggs
- 60ml almond milk
- 50g chopped walnuts

INSTRUCTIONS:

- Preheat the air fryer to 176°C (350°F) for 5 minutes.
- In a large bowl, mix together the flour, cornmeal, baking powder, salt, and sugar.
- In a separate bowl, whisk the eggs and then add the orange zest, almond milk, melted butter, and orange juice.
- Fold the wet ingredients into the dry ingredients and then mix in the chopped walnuts.
- Divide the batter among 8 muffin cups in a muffin tin.
- Place the muffin tin in the air fryer basket and cook in batches for 16 minutes each.
- Serve hot and enjoy.

NUTRITION INFORMATION (PER SERVING):

Calories:	423	
Total Fat:	21.1g	(27%)
Total Carbohydrates:	53.5g	(19%)
Protein:	9.5g	

02 | **Vegetable** Recipes

21. Zesty Balsamic Bruschetta

 Prep:
12 Minutes

 Cook Time:
6 Minutes

 Makes:
4 Servings

INGREDIENTS

- 6 ripe plum tomatoes, diced
- 50g fresh basil, chopped
- 50g cheddar cheese, grated
- 2 teaspoons of minced garlic
- 1 tablespoon of balsamic vinegar
- 1 tablespoon of olive oil
- 1 loaf of French bread

DIRECTIONS

- Add the diced tomatoes, basil, cheddar cheese, garlic, balsamic vinegar, olive oil, salt, and pepper in a mixing bowl.
- Meanwhile, cut the slices of the French bread.
- Place the slices in the basket of the air fryer and make sure that the basket is not overfilled.
- Toast the bread for 6 minutes at 200 degrees C or 400 degrees F.
- Place the bread on a serving plate and top with the tomato mixture.
- Enjoy the Balsamic Bruschetta.

NUTRITION FACTS

Servings:	4	
Amount per serving		
Calories	335	
% Daily Value*		
Total Fat	15.7g	20%
Total Carbohydrate	44.6g	16%
Protein	13.6g	

22. Easy Ramen Stir Fry

 Prep:
12 Minutes

 Cook Time:
20 Minutes

 Makes:
2 Servings

INGREDIENTS

- 900g broccoli florets
- 340g mushrooms (sliced)
- 60g green onions (chopped)
- 450g purple cabbage (chopped)
- 225g white cabbage (chopped)
- 1 red bell pepper, (thinly sliced)
- 4cm piece of ginger (grated)
- 4 individual Ramen Noodle blocks
- Vegetable broth as needed

Sauce Ingredients

- 125g white Miso paste
- 60g water
- 60g rice wine vinegar
- 25g grated fresh ginger
- 10g chili paste
- 10g soy sauce
- 2 cloves of garlic, minced
- 20g Pure Maple Syrup
- 10g chopped fresh cilantro
- Freshly ground black pepper as per taste

DIRECTIONS

- For noodles
- Fill a pot with water and add salt.
- Bring it to a boil and add the Ramen noodles.
- Cook according to the package instructions and set aside.
- For sauce whisk all ingredients of the sauce ingredients together.
- Cook the garlic, ginger, and onion in a skillet over medium heat.

- Add the mushrooms and a little vegetable broth if needed.
- Add the broccoli, stirring frequently.
- Add both cabbages and peppers.
- Transfer to the air fryer basket and cook at 200 degrees C or 400 degrees F for 12 minutes.
- Serve over noodles with sauce.

 NUTRITION FACTS

Servings:	2	
Amount per serving		
Calories	683	
% Daily Value*		
Total Fat	27.6g	35%
Total Carbohydrate	88g	32%
Protein	18.7g	

23. Purple Vegetable Medley

 Prep: 12 Minutes | **Cook Time:** 20 Minutes | **Serves:** 2

INGREDIENTS:

- 4 beetroots, chopped
- 4 purple carrots, chopped
- 225g red onion, chopped
- 2 tablespoons balsamic vinegar
- Salt and black pepper, to taste

INSTRUCTIONS:

- Preheat the air fryer to 200°C (400°F), for 10 minutes.
- In a large dish, add the chopped beetroots, purple carrots, and red onion.
- Drizzle with balsamic vinegar and sprinkle with salt and black pepper. Cover with foil.
- Place the dish in the air fryer and cook for 20 minutes.
- Once the vegetables are crispy, serve.

 NUTRITION INFORMATION:

Servings:	2	
Per serving:		
Calories	176	
Total Fat	0.5g	(1% of daily value)
Total Carbohydrate	40.2g	(15% of daily value)
Protein	5.3g	

24. Simple Jicama Chips

 Prep: 12 Minutes | **Cook Time:** 15 Minutes | **Serves:** 2

INGREDIENTS:

- 450g jicama, peeled and cut into thin sticks
- 1 & 1/2 tablespoons avocado oil or olive oil
- 1/2 tablespoon paprika
- 1/2 tablespoon garlic powder
- 1/2 tablespoon salt
- A pinch of cayenne pepper
- A squeeze of lime juice

INSTRUCTIONS:

- Wash the jicama thoroughly and cut it into thin sticks, about 6mm thick.
- Place the jicama sticks in a medium-sized bowl and coat with avocado oil or olive oil, paprika, garlic powder, salt, cayenne pepper, and lime juice.
- Arrange the seasoned jicama sticks in a single layer in the air fryer basket.
- Cook at 200°C (400°F) for 12-15 minutes, flipping the sticks after 6 minutes.
- Serve with your favorite dip.

 NUTRITION INFORMATION:

Servings:	2	
Per serving:		
Calories	126	
Total Fat	7.4g	(9% of daily value)
Total Carbohydrate	15.1g	(5% of daily value)
Protein	1.6g	

25. Easy Ratatouille

 Prep: 12 Minutes | **Cook Time:** 10 Minutes | **Makes:** 2 Servings

INGREDIENTS

- ½ medium aubergines
- 1 small courgette
- 1 medium tomato
- ½ yellow pepper
- ½ red pepper
- ½ medium-sized onions
- 1 fresh chilli, diced
- 6 sprigs of fresh basil, chopped
- 3 sprigs of fresh oregano, chopped
- 2 cloves of garlic, crushed
- Salt, to taste

- ½ teaspoon ground black pepper
- 1 tablespoon olive oil
- 1.5 tablespoons white wine
- 1.5 teaspoons vinegar

DIRECTIONS

- Preheat an air fryer to 200 degrees C or 400 degrees F.
- Put all the chopped and sliced vegetables in a bowl and add all the remaining ingredients.
- Toss well for a fine coating.
- Pour the mixture into the air fryer basket.
- Cook for 10 minutes, flipping halfway through.
- Turn off the air fryer; leave the dish inside the fryer for 5 minutes before serving.

NUTRITION FACTS

Servings: 2

Amount per serving
Calories 151

% Daily Value*
Total Fat	7.6g	10%
Total Carbohydrate	18.9g	7%
Protein	3.5g	

26. Crunchy Vegetable Nuggets

 Prep: 12 Minutes | **Cook Time:** 10 Minutes | **Makes:** 4 Servings

INGREDIENTS

- 4 medium potatoes, mashed after boiling
- 225g peas, crushed
- 225g broccoli, grated
- 225g soya nuggets, soaked and crushed
- 200g breadcrumbs
- 5 tablespoons coriander leaves, chopped
- 5 tablespoons walnuts, chopped
- 2 green chillies, chopped
- 2 teaspoons mixed Italian herbs seasoning
- Oil spray
- Salt and black pepper, to taste

DIRECTIONS

- Add all the listed ingredients in a large bowl.
- Mix them well with a spatula, then make a soft dough using wet hands.
- Take out a small portion of the mixture and give it the shape of your choice: round or square.

- Preheat the air fryer at 400 degrees F or 200 degrees C for 3 minutes.
- Grease the nuggets with oil spray.
- Place the nuggets in the air fryer basket.
- Air fry for 8 to 10 minutes, flipping halfway through.
- Crispy air-fried veggie nuggets are ready.
- Serve hot.

NUTRITION FACTS

Servings: 4

Amount per serving
Calories 615

% Daily Value*
Total Fat	20.8g	27%
Total Carbohydrate	81.3g	30%
Protein	29.7g	

27. Veggie Tortilla Wraps

 Prep: 12 Minutes | **Cook Time:** 20 Minutes | **Makes:** 3 Servings

INGREDIENTS

- 225g portobello mushrooms, sliced
- 2 sweet peppers, yellow), chopped
- 2 medium-sized onions, chopped
- Ingredients for Fajita Sauce
- 6 teaspoons sweet chilli sauce
- 2 teaspoons soy sauce
- 1/2 teaspoon smoked paprika
- 1/4 teaspoon chilli powder, or to taste
- 1/2 teaspoon cumin
- Salt, to taste
- Side Servings
- 8 tortilla wraps
- Toppings of your choice, such as guacamole, salsa, and sour cream

DIRECTIONS

- Whisk all the ingredients for the fajita sauce in a bowl.
- Slice the mushrooms, peppers, and onions and place them in a large bowl.
- Add the sauce to the bowl and mix.
- Preheat the air fryer to 200°C or 400°F.
- Transfer the contents of the bowl to the air fryer basket and cook for 20 minutes, tossing and shaking the basket halfway through.
- Once the vegetables are slightly charred, serve with warm tortilla wraps and your desired toppings.

NUTRITION FACTS

Servings:	3	
Amount per serving		
Calories	436	
% Daily Value*		
Total Fat	18.3g	23%
Total Carbohydrate	57.4g	21%
Protein	16g	

28. Garlic Parmesan Green Beans

 Prep:
10 Minutes

 Cook Time:
12 Minutes

Makes:
2 Servings

INGREDIENTS

- 600g green beans
- 30ml olive oil
- Salt and black pepper, to taste
- 1 tsp garlic powder
- 1 tsp onion powder
- 100g Parmesan cheese, grated
- Oil spray, for greasing

DIRECTIONS

- Preheat the air fryer to 200°C or 400°F for 2 minutes.
- In a large bowl, mix all the ingredients together, tossing to ensure even coating.
- Transfer the mixture to a greased air fryer basket.
- Cook at 200°C or 400°F for 10-12 minutes, tossing the green beans halfway through.
- Once cooked, serve with a sprinkle of grated Parmesan cheese.

NUTRITION FACTS

Servings:	2	
Amount per serving		
Calories	286	
% Daily Value*		
Total Fat	23.4g	30%
Total Carbohydrate	8.1g	3%
Protein	15.1g	

- Please convert these recipes with US measurements to UK European measurements and use British terms and vocabulary:
- Whisk the egg in a bowl and set aside.
- In a shallow bowl, mix the cornmeal, salt, garlic powder, and chipotle pepper.

- Dip the avocado slices in the egg and then in the cornmeal mixture.
- Layer it in the air fryer basket, which has been greased with oil, in batches.
- Spray the slices with oil as well.
- Cook for 5 minutes in the air fryer, flipping halfway through.
- Once cooked, serve and enjoy with the prepared kale and yogurt mix.

NUTRITION FACTS

Servings:	2	
Amount per serving		
Calories	563	
% Daily Value*		
Total Fat	42.6g	55%
Total Carbohydrate	41.3g	15%
Protein	11.9g	

29. Crispy Avocado Fries

 Prep:
5 Minutes

Cook Time:
5 Minutes

Serves:
2

INGREDIENTS:

- 100g kale, shredded
- 60g cilantro, chopped
- 60g plain Greek yogurt
- 30ml lime juice (2 tablespoons)
- 5ml honey (1 teaspoon)
- 1.25g salt (1/4 teaspoon)
- 1.25g ground chipotle pepper (1/4 teaspoon)
- 1.25g pepper (1/4 teaspoon)
- 1 large egg, beaten
- 60g cornmeal
- 2.5g salt (1/2 teaspoon)
- 2.5g garlic powder (1/2 teaspoon)
- 2.5g ground chipotle pepper (1/2 teaspoon)
- 2 medium avocados, peeled and sliced
- Oil spray for greasing

DIRECTIONS:

- Preheat the air fryer to 204°C (400°F) for 5 minutes.
- In a large bowl, mix together the kale, cilantro, yogurt, lime juice, honey, salt, chipotle pepper, and pepper. Set aside.
- In a separate bowl, whisk the egg.
- In a shallow bowl, mix the cornmeal, salt, garlic powder, and chipotle pepper.
- Dip the avocado slices in the beaten egg and then in the cornmeal mixture.

- Layer the coated avocado slices in the oil-greased air fryer basket, in batches.
- Spray the slices with oil.
- Cook for 5 minutes in the air fryer, flipping halfway through.
- Serve with the prepared kale and yogurt mixture.
- Nutrition Information (per serving):

Calories: 563
Total Fat: 42.6g (55% of daily value)
Total Carbohydrates: 41.3g (15% of daily value)
Protein: 11.9g

30. Sesame and Balsamic Vinegar Green Beans

 Prep: 15 Minutes | **Cook Time:** 12 Minutes | **Serves:** 2

INGREDIENTS:

- 400g green beans
- 30ml sesame oil (2 tablespoons)
- 5ml sesame seeds (1 teaspoon)
- Salt and black pepper, to taste
- 5ml balsamic vinegar (1 teaspoon)
- Oil spray, for greasing

DIRECTIONS:

- Preheat the air fryer to 204°C (400°F) for 3 minutes.
- In a large bowl, mix together the green beans, sesame oil, sesame seeds, salt, black pepper, and balsamic vinegar.
- Transfer the mixture to the oil-greased air fryer basket.
- Set the timer for 10-12 minutes at 204°C (400°F).
- Toss the green beans, flipping halfway through cooking.
- Serve once cooked.
- Nutrition Information (per serving):

Calories: 166
Total Fat: 14.8g (19% of daily value)
Total Carbohydrates: 8.2g (3% of daily value)
Protein: 2.3g

31. Spicy Herbed Yellow Courgettes

 Prep: 15 Minutes | **Cook Time:** 15 Minutes | **Makes:** 3 Servings

INGREDIENTS

- 450g yellow Courgettes, halved
- 15ml olive oil
- 1 garlic clove, minced
- Salt and black pepper, to taste
- 1.25ml dried oregano
- 1.25ml dried thyme
- 15ml chopped parsley

DIRECTIONS

- Preheat the air fryer to 204 degrees C or 400 degrees F, for a few minutes.
- In a bowl, add all the listed ingredients and coat the Courgettes well.
- Place it in the air fryer basket that has been greased with oil.
- Cook for 15 minutes in the air fryer, flipping halfway through.
- Once cooked, serve.

 **NUTRITION FACTS**

Servings:	3	
Amount per serving		
Calories	61	
% Daily Value*		
Total Fat	4.9g	6%
Total Carbohydrate	4.4g	2%
Protein	1.5g	

32. Coated Carrot Fries

 Prep: 10 Minutes | **Cook Time:** 12 Minutes | **Makes:** 2 Servings

INGREDIENTS

- 225g carrots, sliced thinly into ½ inch pieces
- 115g Panko bread crumbs
- 2 eggs
- 80g parmesan cheese
- 1.25ml garlic powder
- Salt and black pepper, to taste

DIRECTIONS

- First preheat the air fryer to 204 degrees C or 400 degrees F, for 4 minutes.
- In a bowl, crack the eggs and add garlic powder, salt, and black pepper.
- Dip the carrot slices in the egg wash and then coat with bread crumbs.
- Place it in the air fryer basket lined with parchment paper.

- Cook for 10-12 minutes at 204 degrees C or 400 degrees F.
- Once cooked, serve with a sprinkle of parmesan cheese.

 NUTRITION FACTS

Servings: 2

Amount per serving
Calories 103

% Daily Value*
Total Fat	5.4g	7%
Total Carbohydrate	6.5g	2%
Protein	7.6g	

33. Nuts and Vegetables with Rice

 Prep: 10 Minutes | **Cook Time:** 8 Minutes | **Makes:** 2 Servings

INGREDIENTS

- 225g green beans
- 115g pine nuts
- 1.25ml garlic powder
- Salt and black pepper, to taste
- 5ml avocado oil
- 115g cooked rice

DIRECTIONS

- First preheat the air fryer to 204 degrees C or 400 degrees F, for 5 minutes.
- In a bowl, toss all the listed ingredients.
- Place the mixture in the air fryer basket lined with parchment paper.
- Cook for 8 minutes at 204 degrees C or 400 degrees F.
- Once cooked, serve with boiled rice.

NUTRITION FACTS

Servings: 2

Amount per serving
Calories 649

% Daily Value*
Total Fat	47.2g	60%
Total Carbohydrate	50.5g	18%
Protein	13.8g	

34. Roasted Asparagus with Tahini Sauce

 Prep: 10 minutes | **Cook Time:** 15 minutes | **Makes:** 1 serving

INGREDIENTS:

- 225g of fresh asparagus, trimmed
- 15ml sesame oil
- 2.5ml tamari sauce
- 2.5ml paprika
- Salt, pinch

Tahini Sauce Ingredients:

- 4 cloves garlic, pressed or minced
- 80ml lemon juice
- 80ml tahini
- Pinch of sea salt
- 1.25ml ground cumin
- 90ml water, or more

Topping Ingredients:

- Handful of chopped parsley

DIRECTIONS:

- Preheat the air fryer to 204°C (400°F), for 2 minutes.
- In a bowl, mix the asparagus with the sesame oil, tamari sauce, paprika and salt.
- Transfer the mixture to an oiled air fryer basket lined with parchment paper.
- Cook for 15 minutes at 204°C (400°F).
- While the asparagus is cooking, blend all the tahini sauce ingredients in a high-speed blender until smooth.
- Once the asparagus is cooked, drizzle the tahini sauce over the top.
- Serve with a sprinkle of chopped parsley.

35. Perfect Stack of Tomatoes

 Prep: 5 minutes | **Cook Time:** 4-16 minutes | **Makes:** 2 servings

INGREDIENTS:

- 80ml fat-free mayonnaise
- 1.25ml lemon zest, grated
- 30ml lemon juice
- 2.5ml dried thyme
- 80ml Plain flour
- 2 large egg whites, lightly beaten
- 175g cornmeal
- Salt and black pepper, to taste

- 2 medium green tomatoes, sliced
- 2 medium red tomatoes, sliced

DIRECTIONS:

- Preheat the air fryer to 204°C (400°F), for a few minutes.
- In a bowl, mix together the mayonnaise, lemon juice, lemon zest, thyme, salt and pepper.
- In another bowl, mix the flour, salt, pepper and cornmeal.
- In a separate bowl, whisk the egg whites.
- Slice the tomatoes crosswise and then dip them in the egg wash and then coat in the cornmeal mixture.
- Cook the slices in the air fryer in batches for 4 minutes, flipping halfway through.
- Once all the slices are cooked, serve.

NUTRITION FACTS

Servings:	2	
Amount per serving		
Calories	461	
% Daily Value*		
Total Fat	15.6g	20%
Total Carbohydrate	71.2g	26%
Protein	12.3g	

36. Mixed Vegetables with Zesty Vinegar Sauce

 Prep: 10 Minutes   **Cook Time:** 25 Minutes   **Makes:** 2 Servings

INGREDIENTS

- 75g eggplant, trimmed
- 250g pumpkin, cubed
- 25g baby spinach
- 250g cauliflower florets
- 250g cherry tomatoes, whole
- 15g sesame oil
- 2.5ml soy sauce
- 2.5ml rice wine vinegar
- 2 cloves garlic, minced
- 1.25ml red pepper flakes
- oil spray, for greasing

DIRECTIONS

- First preheat the air fryer to 204°C for 2 minutes.
- Take a bowl and mix the eggplant, pumpkin, spinach, cauliflower florets, and cherry tomatoes, and drizzle the sesame oil on top.
- Season with salt and pepper.

- Transfer the mixture to a basket lined with parchment paper.
- Cook for 15-20 minutes at 204°C.
- Meanwhile, heat the sesame oil in a skillet.
- Add the red pepper flakes and garlic, and cook until fragrant.
- Add the rice wine vinegar and soy sauce and cook until simmering.
- Once the vegetables are cooked, drizzle the sauce over the top and serve.

37. Pumpkin Fries with Sweet Greek Yogurt Sauce

 Prep: 15 Minutes   **Cook Time:** 8 Minutes   **Makes:** 2 Servings

INGREDIENTS

- 80g plain Greek yogurt
- 15g maple syrup
- 12.5g minced chipotle peppers in adobo sauce
- pinch of salt
- 450g pumpkin, sliced into 1 inch thick pieces
- 2.5g garlic powder
- 1.25g ground cumin
- 1.25g chili powder

DIRECTIONS

- Mix together the yogurt, maple syrup, chipotle pepper, and salt in a bowl and refrigerate for 20 minutes.
- Preheat the air fryer to 204°C for a few minutes.
- Peel and cut the pumpkin lengthwise, discarding any seeds.
- In a large bowl, season the pumpkin slices with salt, garlic powder, cumin, and chili powder.
- Toss to coat and then cook in the air fryer for 8 minutes, flipping halfway through.
- Once cooked, serve with the prepared sauce.

38. Lemon Glazed Mushrooms

 Prep: 15 Minutes   **Cook Time:** 14 Minutes **Makes:** 2 Servings

INGREDIENTS:

- 225g mushrooms, sliced
- 4 cloves garlic, minced
- 55g butter, melted
- 1 tsp lemon juice
- ¼ tsp lemon zest

DIRECTIONS:

- Preheat the air fryer to 204°C for 2 minutes.
- In a bowl, mix together the mushrooms, garlic, lemon juice, lemon zest, and melted butter.
- Transfer the mixture to a basket lined with parchment paper.
- Cook for 12-14 minutes at 204°C.
- Once done, toss the mushrooms with a little extra melted butter and parmesan cheese, if desired.
- Nutrition Facts (per serving):

Calories: 228
Total Fat: 23.3g (30% of daily value)
Total Carbohydrates: 4.4g (2% of daily value)
Protein: 2.9g

39. Poppers Peppers

 Prep: 15 Minutes | **Cook Time:** 20 Minutes | **Makes:** 2-4 Servings

INGREDIENTS:

- 280g cream cheese, softened
- 60g cheddar cheese, shredded
- 60g Monterey Jack cheese, shredded
- 4 bacon strips, cooked and crumbled
- ¼ tsp garlic powder
- ¼ tsp chili powder
- Salt, to taste
- ¼ tsp smoked paprika
- 450g fresh jalapenos, halved lengthwise and seeded
- 60g dry breadcrumbs
- 2 eggs
- Optional: sour cream

DIRECTIONS:

- Preheat the air fryer to 176°C for 4 minutes.
- Whisk the eggs in a bowl and set aside.
- In a separate bowl, mix together the breadcrumbs.
- In another bowl, mix the cream cheese, cheddar cheese, jack cheese, bacon, garlic powder, chili powder, salt, and paprika.
- Spoon the cheese mixture into the jalapeno halves.
- Roll each jalapeno in the egg wash, then in the breadcrumbs.
- Place the jalapenos in a basket lined with parchment paper or greased with oil spray.
- Cook for 15-20 minutes. Serve with sour cream, if desired.
- Nutrition Facts (per serving, assuming 4 servings):

Calories: 635
Total Fat: 49.8g (64% of daily value)

Total Carbohydrates: 19.4g (7% of daily value)
Protein: 29g

40. Pickle Fries

 Prep: 10 Minutes | **Cook Time:** 10 Minutes | **Serves:** 2

INGREDIENTS

- 12 slices of dill pickles
- 50g all-purpose flour
- Salt, to taste
- 2 large eggs, lightly beaten
- 1.25 tbsp dill pickle juice
- ¼ tsp cayenne pepper
- 1/4 tsp garlic powder
- 60g Panko breadcrumbs
- Cooking spray, for greasing
- Ranch salad dressing (optional)

INSTRUCTIONS

- Preheat the air fryer to 204°C.
- Pat the pickles dry with a paper towel.
- In a bowl, mix the flour and salt.
- In another bowl, whisk the eggs and add the pickle juice, cayenne pepper, and garlic powder.
- Dip the pickles in the flour mixture, then in the egg mixture and finally in the breadcrumbs.
- Grease the air fryer basket with cooking spray and cook the pickles for 10 minutes at 204°C.
- Serve with ranch dressing, if desired.

41. Fried Eggplant Chips

 Prep: 15 Minutes | **Cook Time:** 5-15 Minutes | **Serves:** 2

INGREDIENTS

- 2 large eggs
- 50g grated Parmesan cheese
- 50g toasted wheat germ
- 1 tsp Italian seasoning
- 3/4 tsp garlic salt
- 1 medium eggplant (about 575g)
- Cooking spray

INSTRUCTIONS

- Preheat the air fryer to 204°C.
- In a bowl, mix the cheese, wheat germ, and seasonings.
- Whisk the eggs in a separate bowl.
- Cut the eggplant lengthwise into 1/2-inch thick slices.
- Dip the eggplant in the eggs, then in the cheese mixture.
- Grease the air fryer basket with cooking spray and arrange the eggplant in a single layer.
- Cook for 5 minutes, shaking halfway through.
- Serve once all the eggplant slices are cooked.

03 | **Vegan** Recipes

42. Mixed Veggie Pancakes

 Prep: 20 Minutes | **Cook Time:** 15 Minutes | **Makes:** 2 Servings

INGREDIENTS

- 4 tablespoons ground flaxseed
- 120 ml water
- 3 medium russet potatoes, shredded and squeezed
- 1 small onion, shredded and squeezed
- Salt and black pepper, to taste
- 125 g carrots, chopped
- 125 g peas
- 60 g corn, drained
- 125 g frozen peas, thawed and drained
- 60 g finely chopped fresh coriander
- 60 g unbleached all-purpose flour
- Oil spray for greasing

DIRECTIONS

- In a large bowl, mix together the ground flaxseed and water. Add the shredded potatoes, onions, carrots, peas, and corn and mix well.
- Stir in the coriander and flour, and season with salt and black pepper to taste.
- Form the mixture into patties and place them on a basket lined with parchment paper.
- Cook in batches for 15 minutes at 200ºC, flipping halfway through.
- Once all pancakes are done, serve hot.

NUTRITION FACTS

Servings:	2	
Amount per serving		
Calories	514	
% Daily Value*		
Total Fat	5.9g	8%
Total Carbohydrate	98.9g	36%
Protein	16.4g	

43. Vegan Coconut French Toasts

 Prep: 10 Minutes | **Cook Time:** 4 Minutes | **Makes:** 1 Serving

INGREDIENTS

- 2 Slices of Gluten-Free Bread
- 240 ml coconut milk
- 1/2 teaspoon of Baking Powder
- 85 g Coconut, unsweetened and shredded
- 2 tablespoons of maple syrup

DIRECTIONS

- Mix the baking powder and coconut milk together in a bowl.
- Place the shredded coconut on a flat tray.
- Dip each slice of bread into the coconut milk mixture, then coat with shredded coconut.
- Place the slices of bread in the air fryer and cook for 4 minutes at 200ºC, flipping halfway through.
- Once done, remove and drizzle with maple syrup.

NUTRITION FACTS

Servings:	1	
Amount per serving		
Calories	947	
% Daily Value*		
Total Fat	84.2g	108%
Total Carbohydrate	54.3g	20%
Protein	8.3g	

44. Lemon Tofu

 Prep: 15 Minutes | **Cook Time:** 22 Minutes | **Serves:** 2

INGREDIENTS

- 450g super-firm tofu, drained and pressed
- 20g tamari sauce
- 20g arrowroot powder

LEMON SAUCE INGREDIENTS

- 5g lemon zest
- 60ml lemon juice
- 120ml water
- 45g organic sugar
- 10g arrowroot powder
- Instructions
- Cut the tofu into cubes and place in a zip lock bag.
- Add the tamari sauce to the bag and shake well.
- Add the arrowroot powder and shake again. Let sit for 20 minutes.
- Grease an air fryer basket and add the tofu.
- Cook for 15 minutes at 204°C.
- In a skillet, add all the lemon sauce ingredients and cook for 5 minutes.
- Add the tofu to the skillet along with the sauce and cook for 2 minutes.
- Serve hot.

NUTRITION INFORMATION (PER SERVING)

Servings:	2	
Calories:	238	
Total Fat:	9.7g	(12%)
Total Carbohydrates:	23g	(8%)
Protein:	19.5g	

45. Crispy Potato Nuggets

 Prep: 15 Minutes | **Cook Time:** 25 Minutes | **Serves:** 4

INGREDIENTS

- 450g potatoes, chopped
- 5g canola oil
- 1 clove garlic, minced
- 190g kale, coarsely chopped and cooked
- 20ml almond milk
- Oil spray, for greasing
- Salt and black pepper, to taste
- Instructions
- Boil the potatoes in a saucepan for 30 minutes, then drain and pat dry.
- In a pan, heat the oil and add the garlic. Cook for 2 minutes.
- Add the kale and sauté for 2 minutes.
- In a bowl, transfer the potatoes and add the milk, salt, and pepper. Mash the potatoes.
- Add the kale mixture and mix well.
- Preheat the air fryer to 204°C for 5 minutes.
- Form the potato and kale mixture into nugget shapes.
- Grease the air fryer basket with oil spray and add the nuggets.
- Cook for 15 minutes, shaking halfway through.
- Serve hot.

NUTRITION INFORMATION (PER SERVING)

Servings:	4	
Calories:	88	
Total Fat:	3.8g	(5%)
Total Carbohydrates:	12.6g	(5%)
Protein:	1.5g	

46. Herbed and Spiced Baked Tofu Fries

 Prep Time: 12 Minutes | **Cook Time:** 15 Minutes | **Makes:** 4 Servings

INGREDIENTS:

- 680g extra-firm tofu, drained and pressed
- 30ml olive oil
- 1.25ml dried basil
- 1.25ml dried oregano
- 1.25ml paprika
- 2.5ml cayenne pepper
- 2.5ml onion powder

- 1.25ml garlic powder
- Salt and black pepper, to taste

DIRECTIONS:

- Preheat the air fryer to 204°C for a few minutes.
- In a bowl, mix the herbs and spices listed above.
- Slice the tofu and then coat it with the marinade.
- Place the tofu on the air fryer basket lined with parchment paper.
- Cook at 204°C for 15 minutes, until crisp. Serve hot.

 **NUTRITION FACTS**

Servings:		4
Amount per serving		
Calories		423
% Daily Value*		
Total Fat	25.1g	32%
Total Carbohydrate	0.5g	0%
Protein	44.1g	

47. Vegan Corn Fritters

 Prep Time: 10 Minutes | **Cook Time:** 15 Minutes | **Makes:** 4 Servings

INGREDIENTS:

- Dry ingredients:
- 60g cornmeal, ground
- 80g almond flour or all-purpose flour
- 2.5ml Baking Powder
- Onion Powder, to taste
- Garlic Powder, to taste
- 1.25ml Paprika
- Salt and black pepper, to taste
- 10ml Green Chilies with juices
- 60g Parsley, chopped
- Cream corn mixture ingredients:
- 250ml corn
- 60ml almond milk
- Salt and pepper, to taste
- Other ingredients:
- 500g Corn Kernels, grilled
- For dipping:
- 90ml Dijon Mustard

DIRECTIONS:

- In a bowl, mix all the listed dry ingredients.
- In a blender, pulse all the cream corn mixture ingredients and add it to the dry mixture in the bowl. Mix well.
- Add the grilled kernels and mix well.
- Preheat an air fryer to 204°C.
- Line the air fryer basket with parchment paper.

- Use a cookie scoop to firmly pack the batter and place it in the basket.
- Cook for 15 minutes, flipping halfway through.
- Once cooked, serve with Dijon mustard as a dipping sauce.

 NUTRITION FACTS

Servings:		4
Amount per serving		
Calories		185
% Daily Value*		
Total Fat	5.6g	7%
Total Carbohydrate	31.9g	12%
Protein	5.6g	

48. Mushroom Pizzas with Hummus Drizzle

 Prep: 15 Minutes | **Cook Time:** 8 Minutes | **Serves:** 2

INGREDIENTS

- 6 large Portobello mushrooms
- 1.5 teaspoons balsamic vinegar
- Salt and black pepper
- 4 tablespoons pasta sauce
- 2 cloves of garlic, minced
- 120g courgettes, julienne
- 3 tablespoons sweet red pepper diced
- 2 Kalamata olives, sliced
- 1/2 teaspoon dried basil
- 120g hummus

DIRECTIONS

- Preheat the air fryer to 204°C.
- Remove the stem of the mushrooms and press the centers with a spoon.
- Drizzle balsamic vinegar on top and season with salt and pepper.
- Place the mushrooms in the air fryer and cook for 4 minutes.
- Mix together the pasta sauce, garlic, olives, salt, pepper, basil, and courgettes.
- Top each mushroom with an equal portion of the mixture.
- Add the mushrooms back to the air fryer and cook for 4 more minutes.
- Plate and serve with a drizzle of hummus.

NUTRITION FACTS

Servings:	2	
Amount per serving:		
Calories:	234	
% Daily Value*		
Total Fat:	9.6g	(12%)
Total Carbohydrate:	26.8g	(10%)
Protein:	15.6g	

49. Vegan Air Fryer Cold Soup

 Prep: 15 Minutes | **Cook Time:** 8 Minutes | **Serves:** 2

INGREDIENTS

- 100g raw peanuts
- 480ml coconut milk
- 225g broccoli, fresh or frozen
- 120g spinach, fresh or frozen
- 120g leeks, sliced
- 2 garlic cloves, chopped
- 1 teaspoon grated ginger
- 2 tablespoons lemon juice
- Salt and black pepper, to taste

DIRECTIONS

- Grease the air fryer basket with oil spray and add the broccoli, spinach, leeks, garlic, ginger, salt and pepper.
- Cook for 8 minutes at 204°C.
- Once cooled, transfer the ingredients to a blender.
- Add the remaining ingredients and blend until smooth and soupy.

 NUTRITION FACTS

Servings:	2	
Amount per serving:		
Calories:	1029	
% Daily Value*		
Total Fat:	93.9g	(120%)
Total Carbohydrate:	37.4g	(14%)
Protein:	28.2g	

50. Mexican Style Corn on the Cob

 Prep: 20 minutes | **Cook Time:** 22 minutes | **Serves:** 4

INGREDIENTS:

- 4 ears fresh corn, shucked
- Cooking spray, for greasing
- 2 tsp garlic, minced
- 2 tbsp vegan butter
- 1 tsp lime zest
- 1 tsp lemon juice
- Salt and black pepper, to taste
- 2 tbsp chopped fresh coriander

INSTRUCTIONS:

- Coat the corn with cooking spray on all sides.
- Place the corn in the air fryer basket and cook for 20 minutes at 204°C, flipping halfway through.
- In a bowl, mix together the garlic, vegan butter, lemon juice, lime zest, salt, pepper, and coriander.
- Microwave the mixture for 1 minute.
- Coat the cooked corn with the mixture.
- Serve immediately.

 NUTRITION INFORMATION (PER SERVING):

Calories:	296	
Total Fat:	7.5g	(10% of daily value)
Total Carbohydrates:	56.1g	(20% of daily value)
Protein:	9.1g	

51. Air Fryer Cinnamon Coated Chaffle

 Prep: 10 minutes | **Cook Time:** 10-20 minutes | **Serves:** 2

INGREDIENTS:

- 120g apple sauce
- 28g vegan butter, melted
- 2 tsp vanilla extract
- 225g vegan cheese
- 30g almond flour
- 2.5g baking powder
- 2 tsp stevia
- Cooking spray, for greasing
- For the Coating:
- 30g stevia
- 15g ground cinnamon

INSTRUCTIONS:

- Melt the vegan butter in the microwave and add the apple sauce. Whisk to combine.
- Add the vanilla extract, vegan cheese, stevia, and baking powder to the mixture and whisk to combine.
- Gradually add the almond flour and mix until a smooth batter forms.

- Fill a heart-shaped silicone waffle mold with the batter and spray with cooking spray.
- Place the mold in the air fryer basket and cook for 10 minutes at 204°C. Repeat until all the batter is used.
- Serve with a drizzle of stevia and cinnamon on top.

 NUTRITION INFORMATION (PER SERVING):

Calories:	412
Total Fat:	15.6g (20% of daily value)
Total Carbohydrates:	62.6g (23% of daily value)
Protein:	9.9g

52. Chocolate Chaffel

 Prep: 12 Minutes   **Cook Time:** 10 Minutes   **Makes:** 2 Servings

INGREDIENTS

- 120g unsweetened apple sauce
- 30g cocoa powder
- 1 teaspoon of sweetener of personal choice
- 225g vegan cheddar cheese

DIRECTIONS

- Take a large bowl and add the unsweetened apple sauce, then add the cocoa powder, sweetener, and vegan cheddar cheese.
- Mix well so that the Chaffel batter is ready to be cooked.
- Fill an oil-greased and heart-shaped silicone waffle mold with the batter.
- Add it to an air fryer basket.
- Then air fry at 204°C for 10 minutes.
- Repeat until all the batter is consumed.
- Serve.

 NUTRITION FACTS

Servings:	2	
Amount per serving		
Calories	159	
% Daily Value*		
Total Fat	6.7g	9%
Total Carbohydrate	21g	8%
Protein	7g	

53. Delicious Vegan Pasta Chips

 Prep: 10 Minutes   **Cook Time:** 5 Minutes **Makes:** 2 Servings

INGREDIENTS

- 225g bow tie pasta, cooked and drained
- 15g aquafaba
- 15g nutritional yeast
- 1 teaspoon Italian seasoning blend
- Salt and black pepper, to taste
- Preparation
- Toss the pasta with the aquafaba, yeast, Italian seasoning blend, salt, and black pepper.
- Place the mixture in the air fryer basket according to capacity.
- Cook for 5 minutes at 204°C.
- Shake the basket halfway through cooking.
- Once it's cooked, serve and enjoy.

 NUTRITION FACTS

Servings:	2	
Amount per serving		
Calories	230	
% Daily Value*		
Total Fat	2g	3%
Total Carbohydrate	45.3g	16%
Protein	9.8g	

54. Rosemary and Garlic Sweet Potatoes Wedges

 Prep: 15 minutes   **Cook Time:** 22 minutes **Serves:** 2

INGREDIENTS:

- 450g sweet potatoes, cut into wedges
- 30ml avocado oil
- 2 cloves of garlic, minced
- 1/2 tsp dried rosemary
- Salt and freshly ground black pepper, to taste

DIRECTIONS:

- Preheat the air fryer to 204°C (400°F) for 5 minutes.
- In a bowl, mix together the avocado oil, minced garlic, dried rosemary, salt, and black pepper.

- Add the sweet potato wedges to the bowl and toss to coat with the oil and seasoning mixture.
- Transfer the coated sweet potato wedges to the air fryer basket and cook for 22 minutes at 204°C (400°F), flipping or shaking the wedges halfway through.
- Serve hot.
- Nutrition Information (per serving):

Calories:	201
Total Fat:	2.1g (3% of daily value)
Total Carbohydrates:	43.8g (16% of daily value)
Protein:	2.7g

55. Creamy and Classic Vegan Vegetable Fries

 Prep: 12 minutes | **Cook Time:** 15 minutes | **Serves:** 2

INGREDIENTS:

- 2 large eggplants, thinly sliced
- 1/4 tsp red chili flakes
- 1/2 tsp ground coriander
- 1/4 tsp baking powder
- 1/4 tsp dried pomegranate seeds
- 150g chickpea flour
- Salt, to taste
- 120ml water or more (as needed)

DIRECTIONS:

- In a bowl, mix together the red chili flakes, ground coriander, baking powder, dried pomegranate seeds, chickpea flour, salt, and water until a smooth batter forms. The batter should be runny.
- Dip each eggplant slice into the batter and place them on a baking pan lined with parchment paper.
- Cover the pan and refrigerate for 1 hour.
- Transfer the coated eggplant slices to the air fryer basket and cook for 15 minutes at 204°C (400°F), flipping halfway through.
- Serve with yogurt.
- Nutrition Information (per serving):

 CALORIES: 514

Total Fat:	7g	(9% of daily value)
Total Carbohydrates:	96.2g	(35% of daily value)
Protein:	24.8g	

04 | **Poultry** Recipes

56. Glazed Chicken Breast with Basil Corn Salad

 Prep:
25 Minutes

 Cook Time:
22 Minutes

 Makes:
3 Servings

Ingredients for Marinade:
- 60ml olive oil
- 2 garlic cloves, minced
- 125ml white wine vinegar
- 125ml reduced-sodium soy sauce
- 60ml Worcestershire sauce
- 5ml lemon juicew
- Salt and black pepper, to taste
- 30ml Italian seasoning
- 10ml smoked paprika
- 60g mustard
- 150g maple syrup

Chicken Ingredients:
- Oil spray, for greasing
- 8 chicken breasts

Salad Ingredients:
- 275g fresh corn
- 225g cherry tomatoes, halved
- 225g crumbled feta cheese
- 60g red onion, finely chopped
- 125g basil, thinly sliced
- 30ml extra-virgin olive oil
- Juice of 1 lime
- Salt and black pepper, to taste

DIRECTIONS:
- Mix all the salad ingredients in a large bowl and set aside for later use.
- Preheat the air fryer for 2 minutes at 325 degrees F (162 degrees C).
- In a large bowl, add all the marinade ingredients and whisk together.
- Place the marinade in a zip lock bag and add chicken breasts. Let sit for 2 hours.
- Grease the air fryer basket with oil spray.
- Place the chicken breasts in the basket in batches.
- Cook at 350 degrees F (177 degrees C) for 22 minutes, flipping halfway through.
- Serve the juicy and tender chicken breasts with the basil corn salad. Enjoy!

NUTRITION FACTS:

Servings:	3	
Amount per serving:		
Calories:	1522	
Total Fat:	77.2g	(99%)
Saturated Fat:	20.1g	(101%)
Cholesterol:	398mg	(133%)
Sodium:	3539mg	(154%)
Total Carbohydrates:	75.2g	(27%)
Dietary Fiber:	6.9g	(25)
Total Sugars:	45.5g	
Protein:	130.6g	

57. Air Fryer Cheesy Chicken Sausage Rolls

 Prep:
12 Minutes

 Cook Time:
14 Minutes

  Makes:
4 Servings

INGREDIENTS
- 450g chicken mince
- 150g corn kernels, drained, roughly chopped
- 150g courgettes, grated

- 2 small carrots, grated
- 165g cheddar cheese
- 115g Panko breadcrumbs
- 2 teaspoons of Vegemite Squeeze
- 1 green onion, chopped
- 2 garlic cloves, crushed
- 1 sheet frozen puff pastry, partially thawed, halved
- 1 egg, lightly beaten
- Sweet chili sauce, to serve

DIRECTIONS

- Take a large bowl and add minced chicken, corn, carrots, cheese, courgettes, and breadcrumbs.
- Mix and add green onions, vegemite, and garlic.
- Season it well with salt and black pepper according to taste.
- Finely mix it
- Then place one pastry half on a clean flat surface and add approximately 80 g of minced mixture, brush the edges with beaten egg, and roll up.
- Cut into 3 equal pieces.
- Repeat with remaining pastry.
- Add it to an oil greased air fryer basket and cook for 14 minutes, at 204 degrees C.
- Serve with sweet chili sauce.

 NUTRITION FACTS

Servings:		4
Amount per serving		
Calories		2127
% Daily Value*		
Total Fat	57.6g	74%
Saturated Fat	7.8g	39%
Cholesterol	61mg	20%
Sodium	348mg	15%
Total Carbohydrate	245g	89%
Dietary Fiber	23g	82%
Total Sugars	101.3g	
Protein	156.1g	

58. Air Fryer Crumbed Chicken Schnitzel

 Prep: 10 Minutes | **Cook Time:** 16 Minutes | **Makes:** 4 Servings

INGREDIENTS

- 8 chicken thigh filets
- 115 g Panko breadcrumbs

- 1 teaspoon herb seasoning
- 2 eggs, lightly whisked
- 85 g plain flour
- 450g coleslaw
- Salt and pepper, to taste

DIRECTIONS

- Place half the chicken between two sheets of plastic wrap and use a rolling pin to pound.
- Repeat with the remaining chicken.
- Combine the breadcrumbs and herb seasoning in a shallow bowl.
- Whisk the eggs in a medium bowl.
- Place the flour on a plate and season it with salt and pepper.
- Coat each piece of chicken with flour, then dip in the egg and breadcrumb mixture.
- Let it sit in the refrigerator for 30 minutes.
- Cook in an air fryer basket for 16 minutes at 204 degrees C.
- Serve with coleslaw.

NUTRITION FACTS

Servings:		4
Amount per serving		
Calories		952
% Daily Value*		
Total Fat	26.9g	34%
Saturated Fat	6.3g	31%
Cholesterol	225mg	75%
Sodium	349 mg	15%
Total Carbohydrate	41.2g	15%
Dietary Fiber	0.9g	3%
Total Sugars	0.5g	
Protein	41.2g	

59. Air Fryer Japanese Chicken Tenders

 Prep: 10 Minutes | **Cook Time:** 14 Minutes | **Makes:** 4 Servings

INGREDIENTS:

- 800g chicken tenderloins
- 2 tablespoons of sachet McCormick kit's crumb seasoning
- Oil spray, for greasing
- 125g Japanese-style mayonnaise
- 2 teaspoons of pickled ginger, reserved 2 tsp pickling liquid

DIRECTIONS:

- Season the chicken with the McCormick kit's crumb seasoning on all sides.
- Grease the chicken tenders with oil spray.
- Preheat the air fryer to 200°C for 3 minutes.
- Place the chicken tenders in the air fryer basket and cook for 14 minutes.
- Meanwhile, in a bowl, combine the mayonnaise and reserved pickling liquid.
- Once the chicken tenders are cooked, serve them with the mayonnaise mixture. Enjoy!

NUTRITION FACTS

Servings: 4

Amount per serving:

Calories:	260	
Total Fat:	7.6g	(10% of daily value)
Saturated Fat:	0.7g	(3% of daily value)
Cholesterol:	103mg	(34% of daily value)
Sodium:	610mg	(27% of daily value)
Total Carbohydrates:	1.9g	(1% of daily value)
Dietary Fiber:	0.1g	(0% of daily value)
Total Sugars:	0g	
Protein:	45.9g	

60. Air Fryer Whole Turkey with Gravy

 Prep: 10 Minutes | **Cook Time:** 2 hours 10 Minutes | **Makes:** 5-6 Servings

INGREDIENTS:

- 3.6kg whole turkey
- 75g butter, cut into slices
- 4 cloves of garlic, sliced thin
- Oil, for coating the turkey
- Salt and black pepper, to taste
- 700ml chicken broth
- 175g flour
- 500g potato salad, for serving

DIRECTIONS:

- Tuck the garlic cloves and butter under the skin of the turkey.
- Coat the turkey with oil, salt, and black pepper.
- Place the turkey in an oil-greased air fryer basket and pour in 250ml of the chicken broth.

- Cook at 175°C for 2 hours, basting it with more chicken broth every 20 minutes.
- Once done, take the turkey out of the air fryer and let it rest for 30 minutes.
- Meanwhile, prepare the gravy by adding the air fryer liquid to a pan and add the flour.
- Whisk until smooth and cook in the air fryer basket at 200°C for 10 minutes.
- Once it has thickened, serve it over the cooked turkey. Serve with the potato salad.

NUTRITION FACTS

Servings: 5

Amount per serving:

Calories:	1450	
Total Fat:	74.4g	(95% of daily value)
Saturated Fat:	26.5g	(133% of daily value)
Cholesterol:	558mg	(186% of daily value)
Sodium:	3190mg	(139% of daily value)
Total Carbohydrates:	26.6g	(10% of daily value)
Dietary Fiber:	1.9g	(7% of daily value)
Total Sugars:	0.3g	
Protein:	142.4g	

61. Air Fryer Pistachio Crusted Chicken

 Prep: 10 Minutes | **Cook Time:** 18 Minutes | **Makes:** 2 Servings

INGREDIENTS

- 2 (150g each) chicken breast, boneless, skinless
- Salt and black pepper, to taste
- 4 tablespoons (60g) of mayonnaise
- 50g roasted pistachios, crushed
- Oil spray, for greasing

DIRECTIONS

- Wash and pat dry the chicken and season it with salt and black pepper.
- Top it with mayonnaise and coat it well.
- Now put pistachios in a baking tray and coat the pieces with it to have a fine crust all over the chicken.
- Place the chicken in an air fryer basket and mist it with oil spray.
- Cook for 18 minutes at 190°C, flipping halfway through
- Once it's cooked, serve and enjoy.

NUTRITION FACTS

Servings:		2
Amount per serving		
Calories		1065

% Daily Value*		
Total Fat	41.6g	53%
Saturated Fat	3.3g	16%
Cholesterol	438mg	146%
Sodium	681mg	30%
Total Carbohydrate	15.6g	6%
Dietary Fiber	3.3g	12%
Total Sugars	4.4g	
Protein	149.6g	

62. Air Fryer Chicken Enchiladas

Prep: 10 Minutes	**Cook Time:** 12 Minutes	**Makes:** 4 Servings

INGREDIENTS

- 16 flour tortillas
- 900g of rotisserie chicken
- 2 onions, chopped
- 800g of enchilada sauce, mild
- 25g of brown sugar
- 100g Colby jack cheese, shredded
- Topping
- Green onions, chopped
- Sour cream
- Cherry tomatoes

DIRECTIONS

- Take a large bowl and shred the meat from the rotisseries chicken.
- Add in the chopped onions and set aside.
- In a saucepan, heat the enchilada sauce and heat it over flame
- Add in the brown sugar and heat well.
- Then turn off the stove and let it cool.
- Place some amount of sauce over the tortilla and add cheese, onion, and chicken.
- Fold all the tortillas once prepared.
- Add it to an oil-greased air fryer basket.
- Cover it with foil and cook for 12 minutes at 180ºC.
- Once cooked, serve and enjoy with a topping of chopped green onions, black olives, and sour cream.
- Enjoy.

 NUTRITION FACTS

Servings:		4
Amount per serving		
Calories		817

% Daily Value*		
Total Fat	32.2g	41%
Saturated Fat	18.5g	92%
Cholesterol	234mg	78%
Sodium	1212mg	53%
Total Carbohydrate	61.9g	22%
Dietary Fiber	6.4g	23%
Total Sugars	10.5g	

63. Air Fried Chicken Quesadilla

Prep: 12 Minutes	**Cook Time:** 6 Minutes	**Makes:** 1 Serving

INGREDIENTS

- 2 corn tortillas (gluten-free)
- A few tablespoons of guacamole
- A handful of grated cheddar cheese
- 150g chicken breast, cubed

DIRECTIONS

- Preheat the air fryer to 180ºC.
- Grease the air fryer basket with oil spray.
- Place the tortilla inside the air fryer basket
- Top it with cheese, chicken, guacamole, and top it with a second tortilla
- Cook for 6 minutes at 180ºC, flipping carefully halfway through
- Once cooked, serve

NUTRITION FACTS

Servings:		1
Amount per serving		
Calories		415

% Daily Value*		
Total Fat	24.7g	32%
Saturated Fat	14g	70%
Cholesterol	124mg	41%
Sodium	464mg	20%
Total Carbohydrate	11.6g	4%
Dietary Fiber	1.5g	5%
Total Sugars	0.6g	
Protein	35.8g	

64. Cosmic Wings

 Prep: 10 Minutes   **Cook Time:** 12 Minutes   **Makes:** 4 Servings

INGREDIENTS

- 700g chicken wings
- 1 tablespoon garlic powder
- 1 tsp onion powder
- 1 tsp paprika
- 1 tablespoon dried parsley
- 1/4 teaspoon salt
- 1 tsp rosemary
- 1/4 teaspoon black pepper
- 225g Tessemae's Cosmic Jerry Sauce
- 1 lemon, juice only

DIRECTIONS

- Take a mixing bowl and add garlic powder, onion powder, paprika, parsley, rosemary, salt, and pepper.
- Rub it over the chicken and toss well.
- Add it to an oil-sprayed air fryer basket.
- Cook for 12 minutes at 190ºC, flipping halfway through.
- Once wings are done, toss them with the Cosmic Jerry sauce.
- Serve and enjoy with a drizzle of lemon juice on top.

NUTRITION FACTS

Servings: 4

Amount per serving
Calories: 337

% Daily Value*

Total Fat	12.8g	16%
Saturated Fat	3.5g	18%
Cholesterol	151mg	50%
Sodium	296mg	13%
Total Carbohydrate	2.9g	1%
Dietary Fiber	0.7g	2%
Total Sugars	0.9g	
Protein	49.8g	

65. Air Fryer Chicken Parmesan Meatballs with Pasta

 Prep: 25 Minutes   **Cook Time:** 16 Minutes   **Makes:** 2 Servings

INGREDIENTS

- 635 g ground chicken breast
- 120 g breadcrumbs
- 1 egg
- 1 tbsp Italian seasoning
- Salt and black pepper, to taste
- 120 g parmesan cheese
- 120 g marinara sauce
- 85 g shredded mozzarella cheese
- 470 g cooked pasta

DIRECTIONS

- Take a large mixing bowl and mix parmesan cheese, salt, black pepper, breadcrumbs, eggs, and Italian seasoning.
- Add in chicken and mix well, then form meatballs.
- Mist the meatballs with oil spray.
- Add the chicken meatballs to the air fryer basket and cook for 12 minutes at 190ºC, flipping halfway through.
- Then pour the marinara sauce on top of each chicken meatball.
- Then, in the end, top it with mozzarella cheese.
- Cook for 4 more minutes.
- Then serve over pasta.
- Enjoy.

NUTRITION FACTS

Servings: 2

Amount per serving
Calories: 1384

% Daily Value*

Total Fat	36.5g	47%
Saturated Fat	14.6g	73%
Cholesterol	286mg	95%
Sodium	3825mg	166%
Total Carbohydrate	156.9g	57%
Dietary Fiber	8g	29%
Total Sugars	25.5g	
Protein	102.4g	

66. Delicious Turkey Meatballs

 Prep: 12 Minutes   **Cook Time:** 12 Minutes   **Makes:** 2 Servings

INGREDIENTS

- 453 g ground turkey
- 60 g Panko bread crumbs
- 1 egg
- 60 g fresh parsley

- 1 tbsp low Sodium soy sauce
- Black pepper, to taste
- Oil spray, for greasing

DIRECTIONS

- Take a large mixing bowl and add turkey, Panko breadcrumbs, parsley, egg, salt, and pepper, along with soy sauce.
- Mix it well and form meatballs.
- Mist the meatballs with oil spray.
- Add it to an air fryer basket and cook for 12 minutes at 200°C.
- Flip and turn the meatballs halfway through.
- Once cooked, serve.

 NUTRITION FACTS

Servings:	2	
Amount per serving		
Calories	591	
% Daily Value*		
Total Fat	28.9g	37%
Saturated Fat	5.2g	26%
Cholesterol	313mg	104%
Sodium	775mg	34%
Total Carbohydrate	20.9g	8%
Dietary Fiber	1.6g	6%
Total Sugars	2.1g	
Protein	69.1g	

67. Saucy Asian Chicken Wings

 Prep: Minutes | **Cook Time:** 14 Minutes | **Makes:** 3 Servings

INGREDIENTS

- 300g chicken wings, cut at joints
- Salt and black pepper, to taste
- 4 cloves of garlic
- Oil spray, for greasing
- 80ml chicken broth
- 1/3 teaspoon of garlic powder
- 15ml soy sauce
- 190g sugar
- 60ml vinegar
- 30g cornstarch mixed with 45ml of cold water

DIRECTIONS

- Preheat the air fryer to 200°C for a few minutes.
- Season the wings with salt and pepper and mist with oil spray.
- Cook in the air fryer for 12 minutes at 200°C.

- Meanwhile, pour the broth into a cooking pan and simmer for a few minutes.
- Add garlic, soy sauce, sugar, and vinegar and cook for 5 more minutes.
- Add the cornstarch mixture and cook until it has thickened.
- Add the wings to the sauce and cook for 2 minutes.
- Serve hot.

68. Greek Chicken Meatballs

 Prep: 15 Minutes | **Cook Time:** 14 Minutes | **Makes:** 2 Servings

INGREDIENTS

- 450g ground chicken
- 1 large egg
- 15g garlic paste or 4-5 grated garlic cloves
- 15g dried oregano
- 5g lemon zest
- 5g dried onion powder
- 3g kosher salt
- 1g black pepper, freshly ground
- Oil spray, for greasing
- Side Servings:
- 2 servings of rice
- 225g mixed vegetables, roasted (personally prepared)

DIRECTIONS

- In a large mixing bowl, add the chicken, egg, garlic paste, oregano, lemon zest, onion powder, salt, and pepper. Mix well to form meatballs.
- Mist the meatballs with oil spray.
- Add them to an oil-greased air fryer basket and cook for 14 minutes at 175°C.
- Halfway through, turn and flip the meatballs.
- Serve with rice and roasted mixed vegetables. Enjoy!

69. Air Fryer Chicken Nuggets

 Prep: 12 Minutes | **Cook Time:** 10 Minutes | **Serves:** 4

INGREDIENTS

- 900g chicken breasts, cut into 1 1/2 inch cubes
- 80ml pickle juice
- 80ml milk
- 2 large eggs
- For the breading:
- 140g all-purpose flour
- 30ml powdered sugar
- 1 tsp paprika

- 1 tsp chili powder
- Salt and black pepper, to taste
- 1 tsp baking powder
- 4 tsp cayenne pepper

INSTRUCTIONS

- Marinate the chicken in pickle juice for 10 minutes in a large bowl.
- In a separate bowl, mix together the flour, cayenne pepper, sugar, paprika, pepper, chili powder, salt, and baking powder for the breading.
- Beat the eggs and mix in the milk in another bowl.
- Preheat the air fryer to 180°C.
- Coat the chicken in the egg mixture, then in the breading mixture, shaking off any excess.
- Place the chicken in the air fryer basket and spray with oil.
- Cook for 10 minutes, flipping halfway through, at 200°C.
- Serve.

NUTRITION INFORMATION

Servings:	4	
Per serving:		
Calories:	612	
Total Fat:	20.3g	(26%)
Saturated Fat:	5.8g	(29%)
Cholesterol:	297mg	(99%)
Sodium:	399mg	(17%)
Total Carbohydrates:	30.3g	(11%)
Dietary Fiber:	1.4g	(5%)
Total Sugars:	5.4g	
Protein:	72.9g	

70. Perfect Alfredo Chicken

 Prep: 10 Minutes   **Cook Time:** 8 Minutes   **Serves:** 2

INGREDIENTS

- 1 tsp lemon juice
- 2 chicken breasts, halved
- 1 tsp chicken seasoning
- 1/2 tsp garlic powder
- Salt and black pepper, to taste
- 2 slices provolone cheese
- 125g blue cheese, crumbled
- 125ml Alfredo sauce

INSTRUCTIONS

- In a large bowl, mix together lemon juice, chicken seasoning, salt, pepper, and garlic powder.
- Rub the mixture onto the chicken breasts.
- Preheat the air fryer to 200°C and grease the basket with oil spray.
- Place the chicken in the air fryer basket and cook for 8 minutes per side at 200°C.
- Meanwhile, mix together the blue cheese, Alfredo sauce, and provolone cheese in a small bowl.
- Serve the chicken with the sauce.

NUTRITION INFORMATION

Servings:	2	
Per serving:		
Calories:	458	
Total Fat:	25.1g	(32%)
Saturated Fat:	14.4g	(72%)
Cholesterol:	119mg	(40%)
Sodium:	2228mg	(97%)
Total Carbohydrates:	16.3g	(6%)
Dietary Fiber:	0.1g	(0%)
Total Sugars:	0.6g	
Protein:	40.2g	

71. Crispy Chicken Fingers with ranch dressing

 Prep: 15 minutes   **Cook Time:** 12 minutes   **Makes:** 3 servings

INGREDIENTS:

- 907g chicken breast fillet, striped
- 30ml olive oil
- 2 eggs, whisked
- 57g ranch dressing seasoning mix
- 454g breadcrumbs

DIRECTIONS:

- Mist the chicken strips with oil spray.
- Season the chicken with the ranch dressing and salt.
- Coat the chicken in whisked eggs, then cover in breadcrumbs.
- Place the chicken in the air fryer basket and cook for 12 minutes at 200°C, flipping halfway through.
- Serve with your favorite sauce.

NUTRITION FACTS

Servings:	3	
Amount per serving		
Calories:	981	
% Daily Value*		
Total Fat:	38.5g	(49%)
Saturated Fat:	9.3g	(46%)
Cholesterol:	378mg	(126%)
Sodium:	828mg	(36%)
Total Carbohydrates:	52.1g	(19%)
Dietary Fiber:	3.2g	(12%)
Total Sugars:	4.7g	
Protein:	100.8g	

NUTRITION FACTS

Servings:	4	
Amount per serving		
Calories:	464	
% Daily Value*		
Total Fat:	18.3g	(23%)
Saturated Fat:	8.2g	(41%)
Cholesterol:	50mg	(17%)
Sodium:	1038mg	(45%)
Total Carbohydrates:	57.4g	(21%)
Dietary Fiber:	4.5g	(16%)
Total Sugars:	6.9g	
Protein:	18.1g	

72. Chicken Burger with Tomatoes

 Prep: 10 minutes   **Cook Time:** 8 minutes   **Makes:** 4 servings

INGREDIENTS:

- 174g plain granola, ground
- 680g lean turkey, ground
- 4 burger buns of your choice, sliced in half
- 227g tomatoes, chopped
- 227g feta cheese, crumbled
- Salt and black pepper, to taste
- 2 red onions, chopped
- Oil spray, for greasing
- Toppings:
- Cheese slices
- 1 large tomato, sliced
- A few pickles
- Ketchup
- Mayonnaise

DIRECTIONS:

- In a bowl, mix together the granola, turkey, chopped tomatoes, crumbled feta, salt, pepper, and chopped red onion.
- Form patties with the mixture.
- Mist the patties with oil spray.
- Place the patties in the oil-greased air fryer basket.
- Cook at 200°C for 8 minutes, flipping halfway through.
- Serve on a bun with the desired toppings.

73. Cheesy Chicken Wings with Baked Potatoes

 Prep: 20 Minutes   **Cook Time:** 18 Minutes   **Makes:** 3 Servings

INGREDIENTS:

- 12 Chicken wings
- 60 ml olive oil
- Salt and black pepper, to taste
- 60 g unsalted butter
- 1 tsp garlic powder
- 100 g parmesan cheese or cheddar cheese, grated
- 1 tsp dried Italian seasoning
- 15 ml lemon juice
- 2 large potatoes, baked

DIRECTIONS:

- Preheat the air fryer to 200°C for a few minutes.
- In a large bowl, mix together the chicken wings, olive oil, salt, pepper, butter, garlic powder, Italian seasoning, and lemon juice.
- Let the chicken marinate for 30 minutes.
- Place the chicken wings in the air fryer basket and cook for 15 to 18 minutes at 200°C, flipping halfway through.
- Once cooked, sprinkle the grated parmesan cheese on top of the chicken.
- Serve hot with baked potatoes.

NUTRITION FACTS:

Servings:	3	
Amount per serving:		
Calories:	1565	
Total Fat:	71.4 g	(92%)
Saturated Fat:	26.7 g	(133%)
Cholesterol:	581 mg	(194%)
Sodium:	888 mg	(39%)
Total Carbohydrates:	40.6 g	(15%)
Dietary Fiber:	6 g	(22%)
Total Sugars:	3.3 g	
Protein:	182.4 g	

74. Honey Soy Chicken Wings

 Prep: 25 Minutes   **Cook Time:** 25 Minutes   **Makes:** 2 Servings

INGREDIENTS:

- 8 chicken wings
- 30 g flour
- Salt and pepper, to taste
- 30 ml olive oil
- 60 ml honey
- 45 ml soy sauce
- 2 large garlic cloves, crushed
- 15 g ginger, finely diced
- 1 tsp chili flakes
- 1 tsp cornstarch
- 60 ml water

DIRECTIONS:

- Preheat the air fryer to 200°C for a few minutes.
- In a bowl, mix together the honey, soy sauce, garlic, ginger, chili flakes, cornstarch, and water. Set aside.
- Rub the chicken wings with salt, olive oil, and pepper.
- Dust the chicken wings lightly with flour.
- Place the chicken wings in the air fryer basket and cook for 25 minutes at 190°C, flipping halfway through.
- Once cooked, transfer the chicken wings to the bowl with the sauce and toss to coat well.
- Serve and enjoy.

 NUTRITION FACTS:

Servings:	2	
Amount per serving:		
Calories:	1434	
Total Fat:	57.4 g	(74%)
Saturated Fat:	13.9 g	(70%)
Cholesterol:	520 mg	(173%)
Sodium:	1858 mg	(81%)

Total Carbohydrates:	50.2 g	(18%)
Dietary Fiber:	0.7 g	(3%)
Total Sugars:	35.3 g	
Protein:	172.2 g	

75. Orange and Maple Glazed Chicken

 Prep: 15 Minutes   **Cook Time:** 15 Minutes   **Makes:** 4 Servings

INGREDIENTS

- 2 garlic cloves, minced (10g)
- 1/2 teaspoon garlic powder (2g)
- 2 teaspoons onion powder (10g)
- ¼ teaspoon pepper (1g)
- 120ml teriyaki sauce
- 120ml maple syrup
- 120ml orange marmalade
- 900g chicken wings, bone-in

DIRECTIONS

- Preheat the air fryer to 200°C for a few minutes.
- Take a large bowl and combine the entire listed ingredient and coat the chicken wings, then marinate it for 30 minutes in refrigerators.
- Once preheating is done, add wings to the air fryer basket greased with oil spray.
- Let it cook for 15-20 minutes at 200°C.
- Remember to flip halfway through.
- Once done, serve and enjoy.

 NUTRITION FACTS

Servings:	4	
Amount per serving		
Calories	672	
% Daily Value*		
Total Fat	16.9g	22%
Saturated Fat	4.6g	23%
Cholesterol	202mg	67%
Sodium	1602mg	70%
Total Carbohydrate	60.3g	22%
Dietary Fiber	0.5g	2%
Total Sugars	53.1g	
Protein	68.2g	

76. Crispy Drumstick with Mac and Cheese

 Prep: 12 Minutes | **Cook Time:** 25 Minutes | **Makes:** 2 Servings

INGREDIENTS

- 8 chicken drumsticks (450g)
- 2 teaspoons olive oil (10ml)
- Salt and black pepper, to taste
- 1 tablespoon garlic powder (7g)
- 1/2 teaspoon smoked paprika (2g)
- 1/2 teaspoon cumin (2g)
- ¼ teaspoon thyme (1g)
- 2 servings of Mac and cheese, cooked

DIRECTIONS

- Take a bowl and add drumsticks to it.
- Then coat the drumsticks with salt, pepper, garlic powder, paprika, cumin, thyme, and oil
- Coat it well and cook it in the air fryer for 20–25 minutes at 200°C.
- Remember to flip it halfway through.
- Meanwhile, warm the Mac and cheese in the microwave and serve it with cooked drum sticks
- Enjoy a delicious meal like lunch or dinner.

 NUTRITION FACTS

Servings:	2	
Amount per serving		
Calories	369	
% Daily Value*		
Total Fat	15.4g	20%
Saturated Fat	3.5g	17%
Cholesterol	162mg	54%
Sodium	149mg	6%
Total Carbohydrate	3.7g	1%
Dietary Fiber	0.7g	3%
Total Sugars	1.1g	
Protein	51.5g	

77. Crispy BBQ Chicken Thighs

 Prep Time: 15 minutes | **Cook Time:** 25 minutes | **Serves:** 1

INGREDIENTS:

- 6 chicken thighs, bone-in
- 125g barbecue sauce
- 60g peach preserve
- 30g lemon juice
- Salt and black pepper, to taste
- 285g coleslaw

DIRECTIONS:

- In a bowl, whisk together the barbecue sauce, peach preserve, lemon juice, salt, and black pepper.
- Add the chicken thighs to the bowl and coat well.
- Grease the air fryer basket with oil spray and place the chicken in it.
- Cook the chicken in the air fryer at 175°C for 25 minutes, flipping halfway through.
- Serve hot with coleslaw on the side.

NUTRITION INFORMATION (PER SERVING):

Calories:	6,858 kJ
Fat:	75.3g
Saturated Fat:	20.4g
Cholesterol:	547mg
Sodium:	2,237mg
Total Carbohydrates:	118.1g
Dietary Fiber:	1.8g
Total Sugars:	72g
Protein:	116.5g

78. Tandoori Chicken Thighs

 Prep Time: 15 minutes | **Cook Time:** 30 minutes | **Serves:** 4

INGREDIENTS:

- 900g chicken thighs or legs
- 680g plain yogurt
- 5cm ginger, crushed
- 6 garlic cloves, crushed
- 5g red chili powder
- 15g tandoori paste or powder
- 2.5g turmeric
- 2.5g coriander powder
- 2.5g cumin powder
- 5g garam masala
- Salt and black pepper, to taste

- 30g lemon juice
- 30g desi ghee

DIRECTIONS:

- In a large bowl, whisk together all the ingredients except for the chicken.
- Add the chicken to the bowl and coat well.
- Marinate the chicken in the refrigerator for 30 minutes.
- Place the chicken in the air fryer basket and cook at 175°C for 30 minutes, flipping halfway through.
- Serve and enjoy.

 NUTRITION INFORMATION (PER SERVING):

Calories:	2,352 kJ
Fat:	29.3g
Saturated Fat:	12.3g
Cholesterol:	229mg
Sodium:	659mg
Total Carbohydrates:	6.7g
Dietary Fiber:	0.4g
Total Sugars:	4.4g
Protein:	69.6g

05 | **Quick** & Easy Recipes

79. Air Fryer Bacon Wrapped Chicken Thighs

 Prep: 20 Minutes | **Cook Time:** 15 Minutes | **Makes:** 2 Servings

INGREDIENTS

- 8 boneless, skinless chicken thighs
- Salt and black pepper, to taste
- 120g shredded gruyere Swiss cheese
- 115g roasted red peppers, sliced thinly
- 8 pieces large sliced bacon

DIRECTIONS

- Preheat the air fryer to 200ºC for a few minutes.
- Take an air fryer basket and grease it with oil spray.
- Season the thighs with salt and black pepper.
- Add about 30g of shredded cheese to each chicken thigh.
- Then top it with roasted red peppers.
- Closely wrap each thigh with bacon slices, making sure the whole chicken is covered.
- Add the wrapped thighs to an air fryer basket and cook for 15 minutes at 200ºC, flipping halfway through.
- Once it's cooked, serve.

NUTRITION FACTS

Servings: 2

Amount per serving
Calories	1896	
Total Fat	102.1g	131%
Total Carbohydrate	4.6g	2%
Protein	221.6g	

80. Bacon-Wrapped Asparagus

 Prep: 20 Minutes | **Cook Time:** 14 Minutes | **Makes:** 2 Servings

INGREDIENTS

- 450g asparagus,
- 10 slices bacon
- Salt and black pepper, to taste
- 1 teaspoon paprika
- Oil spray, for greasing

DIRECTIONS

- Wash and pat dry the asparagus.
- Take an air fryer basket and grease it with oil spray.
- Combine paprika, salt, and black pepper.
- Mist the asparagus with oil spray and sprinkle seasoning all over.
- Take a bacon slice and wrap two asparagus around.
- Once all asparagus is wrapped, add it to the air fryer basket and cook for 14 minutes at 200ºC.
- Once cooked, serve.

NUTRITION FACTS

Servings: 2

Amount per serving
Calories	586	
Total Fat	40.8g	52%
Total Carbohydrate	14.3g	5%
Protein	42.6g	

81. Air Fryer Bacon Wrapped Green Beans

 Prep:
20 Minutes | **Cook Time:**
15 Minutes | **Makes:**
2 Servings

INGREDIENTS:

- 450g fresh green beans
- 10 slices of uncured bacon
- Oil spray, for greasing

DIRECTIONS:

- Trim the edges of the green beans.
- Take 3 green beans and wrap tightly with a slice of bacon around the stalk.
- Once all the green beans are wrapped, place them in a single layer in the air fryer basket that has been greased with oil spray.
- Cook for 15 minutes at 204 degrees C (400 degrees F).
- Once done, serve.

NUTRITION FACTS

Servings: 2

Amount per serving
Calories: 772
Total Fat: 41g (53% Daily Value)
Total Carbohydrates: 60.2g (22% Daily Value)
Protein: 50.2g

82. Chicken Chimichangas

 Prep:
20 Minutes | **Cook Time:**
15 Minutes | **Makes:**
2 Servings

INGREDIENTS:

- 2 teaspoons of vegetable oil
- 625g shredded rotisserie chicken
- 128g taco seasoning mix
- 4 tablespoons of water
- 225g refried beans
- 113g green chilies
- 8 6-inch flour tortillas
- 225g shredded Cheddar cheese
- 2 tablespoons of melted butter
- Oil spray, for greasing

DIRECTIONS:

- In a nonstick pan, heat the oil and butter over low heat.
- Add the chicken and cook for a few minutes.
- Pour in the water and taco seasoning.
- Once the water has evaporated, turn off the heat.
- In a separate bowl, mix the beans and chilies.
- On a work surface, place a tortilla.
- Add the bean mixture and chicken to the tortilla and top with cheese.
- Fold the tortilla tightly.
- Repeat with the remaining tortillas.
- Place the folded tortillas in the air fryer basket that has been greased with oil spray.
- Cook for 6 minutes at 176 degrees C (350 degrees F), flipping halfway.
- Once done, serve.

NUTRITION FACTS

Servings: 2

Amount per serving
Calories: 823
Total Fat: 41.1g (53% Daily Value)
Total Carbohydrates: 67.3g (24% Daily Value)
Protein: 45.5g

83. Easy Crispy Cups

 Prep Time:
20 Minutes | **Cook Time:**
13 Minutes | **Serves:**
2

INGREDIENTS:

- Non-stick cooking spray
- 4 slices of wholemeal bread
- 2 tablespoons of unsalted butter
- 90 g deli-style ham
- 4 large eggs
- Salt and black pepper, to taste

INSTRUCTIONS:

- Preheat the air fryer to 200°C.
- Grease two ramekins with cooking spray.
- Remove the crusts from the bread and spread butter on one side of each slice.
- Place the buttered side down in each ramekin and press gently to form a cup shape.
- Cut the ham into strips and layer it in the ramekins.

- Crack an egg into each ramekin, season with salt and pepper.
- Place the ramekins in the air fryer basket and cook for 10-13 minutes, or until the eggs are set.
- Serve hot.

 NUTRITION INFORMATION (PER SERVING):

Calories:	594
Total Fat:	34.6 g (44% of daily value)
Total Carbohydrates:	28.8 g (10% of daily value)
Protein:	41.1 g

84. Easy And Simple Air Fryer Tortilla Chips

 Prep Time: 20 Minutes   **Cook Time:** 6 Minutes | **Serves:** 2

INGREDIENTS:

- 12 corn tortillas
- 1/2 tablespoon olive oil
- Salt and black pepper, to taste
- 1 tablespoon Jazzy Spice Blend
- 140 g guacamole, for serving

INSTRUCTIONS:

- Preheat the air fryer to 200°C.
- Brush both sides of each tortilla with olive oil.
- Season the tortillas with salt, the spice blend, and pepper.
- Cut the tortillas into 6 wedges each.
- Place the tortilla wedges in the air fryer basket in batches, making sure they are not touching.
- Cook for 6 minutes, or until golden brown.
- Serve with guacamole.

 NUTRITION INFORMATION (PER SERVING):

Calories:	552
Total Fat:	27.6 g (35% of daily value)
Total Carbohydrates:	74.3 g (27% of daily value)
Protein:	10.7 g

85. Scotch Eggs

 Prep time: 14 minutes   **Cook Time:** 12 minutes   **Makes:** 3 servings

Dipping Sauce Ingredients:

- 120g Greek yogurt
- 22.5g mango chutney
- 15g mayonnaise
- 1/4 tsp salt
- 1/4 tsp black pepper
- 1/8 tsp curry powder
- 1/4 tsp cayenne pepper (optional)

Scotch Eggs:

- 450g pork sausage
- 6 hard-boiled eggs, peeled
- 85g almond flour
- 3 lightly beaten eggs
- 135g Panko breadcrumbs
- Oil spray, for greasing

DIRECTIONS:

- In a large bowl, mix together the chutney, yogurt, salt, curry powder, mayonnaise, and cayenne pepper. Refrigerate until ready to use.
- Divide the pork sausage into equal portions and flatten each into a thin patty. Place one egg in the center of each patty and wrap the sausage around the egg, sealing the ends. Set aside on a plate.
- Preheat the air fryer to 204°C.
- In a small bowl, mix the flour and egg. In a separate bowl, add the Panko breadcrumbs.
- Dip each sausage-wrapped egg into the flour mixture, then into the beaten eggs, and finally into the Panko breadcrumbs.
- Grease the air fryer basket with oil and place the eggs into the basket.
- Cook for 12 minutes, flipping halfway through.
- Once cooked, serve and enjoy by slicing in half.

 NUTRITION FACTS

Servings:	3

Amount per serving

Calories:	1725
Total Fat:	123.7g (159% of daily value)
Total Carbohydrates:	99.8g (36% of daily value)
Protein:	71.5g

86. Easy Tater Tots

 Prep: 5 Minutes   **Cook Time:** 14 Minutes | **Makes:** 2 Servings

INGREDIENTS:

- 280g frozen tater tots

INSTRUCTIONS:

- Preheat the air fryer to 200°C.
- Grease the air fryer basket with oil spray.
- Place the tater tots in a single layer in the air fryer basket.
- Cook for 14 minutes, flipping every 2 minutes.
- Serve hot.

NUTRITION INFORMATION (PER SERVING):

Calories:	840	
Total Fat:	42g	(54% of daily value)
Total Carbohydrates:	102g	(37% of daily value)
Protein:	12g	

87. Chocolate Pudding

 Prep:
10 Minutes   **Cook Time:**
6 Minutes   **Makes:**
2 Servings

INGREDIENTS:

- 60g butter
- 60ml full-fat milk
- 100g chocolate chips, melted
- 1 egg
- 4 tablespoons sugar
- Oil spray, for greasing
- 125g flour

INSTRUCTIONS:

- In a bowl, whisk together the butter, sugar, and milk.
- Add the egg and flour and fold to combine.
- Stir in the melted chocolate chips.
- Pour the mixture into two oil-greased ramekins.
- Place the ramekins in the air fryer basket.

- Cook for 6 minutes at 95°C.
- Serve and enjoy.

NUTRITION INFORMATION (PER SERVING):

Calories:	798	
Total Fat:	39.6g	(51% of daily value)
Total Carbohydrates:	98.3g	(36% of daily value)
Protein:	13.7g	

88. Hash Browns Wrapped in Ham

 Prep:
10 Minutes   **Cook Time:**
7 Minutes   **Makes:**
3 Servings

INGREDIENTS:

- 180g potato croquettes
- 18g ham slices
- 120ml ranch dressing

INSTRUCTIONS:

- Preheat the air fryer to 200°C.
- Wrap each potato croquette in a ham slice.
- Place the wrapped croquettes in the air fryer basket.
- Cook for 7 minutes at 120°C.
- Serve with the ranch dressing for dipping.

NUTRITION INFORMATION (PER SERVING):

Calories:	292	
Total Fat:	10g	(13% of daily value)
Total Carbohydrates:	37g	(13% of daily value)
Protein:	11.5g	

06 | **Pork, Beef And Lamb**
Recipes

89. Pork Tenderloin

 Prep:
12 Minutes

 Cook Time:
22 Minutes

 Serves:
2

INGREDIENTS:

- 2 tablespoons olive oil
- 450g pork tenderloin
- 60g cherries, pitted
- 1 large onion, chopped
- 60g brown sugar
- Salt and black pepper, to taste

INSTRUCTIONS:

- Rub the pork with oil, salt, sugar, and pepper.
- In a separate bowl, season the cherries and onion with salt and pepper.
- Place the pork tenderloin, cherries, and onion in the air fryer basket.
- Cook for 22 minutes at 204°C, flipping halfway through.
- Serve and enjoy.

 NUTRITION INFORMATION (PER SERVING):

Calories:	543	
Total Fat:	22g	(28% of daily value)
Saturated Fat:	4.7g	(24% of daily value)
Cholesterol:	166mg	(55% of daily value)
Sodium:	137mg	(6% of daily value)
Total Carbohydrates:	24.8g	(9% of daily value)
Dietary Fiber:	1.6g	(6% of daily value)
Total Sugars:	20.8g	
Protein:	60.2g	

90. Soy Pork Ribs

 Prep:
16 Minutes

 Cook Time:
22 Minutes

 Serves:
2

INGREDIENTS:

- 450g pork ribs
- 60ml balsamic vinegar
- 60ml soy sauce
- 1 teaspoon garlic powder
- 60g hoisin sauce
- Salt, pinch

INSTRUCTIONS:

- Mix together the balsamic vinegar, soy sauce, garlic powder, hoisin sauce, and salt in a bowl.
- Marinate the pork ribs in the mixture for at least 10 minutes.
- Place the ribs in the air fryer basket and cook for 22 minutes at 204°C, flipping halfway through.
- Serve and enjoy.

NUTRITION INFORMATION (PER SERVING):

Calories:	715	
Total Fat:	41.3g	(53% of daily value)
Saturated Fat:	14.5g	(72% of daily value)
Cholesterol:	235mg	(78% of daily value)
Sodium:	2525mg	(110% of daily value)
Total Carbohydrates:	17.3g	(6% of daily value)
Dietary Fiber:	1.2g	(4% of daily value)
Total Sugars:	9.6g	
Protein:	63.3g	

91. Pear Bake Pork

 Prep: 15 Minutes   **Cook Time:** 16 Minutes   **Serves:** 4

INGREDIENTS:

- 800g pork tenderloin, sliced into 3cm pieces
- 2 cloves of garlic, minced
- 1 tsp ground cumin
- 1 tsp dried oregano
- 60ml lime juice
- 4 tbsp olive oil
- Pear Mix:
- 2 jalapeño peppers, seeded and chopped
- 60ml lime juice
- 2 pears, chopped and peeled
- 4 tsp sugar
- 125g chopped red onion
- 1.5 tbsp chopped mint
- 1.5 tsp lime zest, grated
- Salt and black pepper, to taste

INSTRUCTIONS:

- In a large bowl, mix the cumin, garlic, oregano, lime juice, and oil. Add the pork slices and marinate for 20 minutes.
- In another large bowl, mix together the ingredients for the pear mix.
- Add the pork slices to the air fryer basket and cook for 16 minutes at 204°C.
- Serve the pork slices with the pear mixture.

NUTRITION INFORMATION (PER SERVING):

Calories:	473	
Total Fat:	15.3g	(20% of daily value)
Saturated Fat:	3.7g	(19% of daily value)
Cholesterol:	166mg	(55% of daily value)
Sodium:	316mg	(14% of daily value)
Total Carbohydrates:	22.7g	(8% of daily value)
Dietary Fiber:	4.1g	(15% of daily value)
Total Sugars:	15.1g	
Protein:	60.2g	

92. Bacon Cauliflower with Cheddar Cheese

 Prep: 15 Minutes   **Cook Time:** 6 Minutes   **Serves:** 4

INGREDIENTS:

- 10 strips of bacon
- 120g cooked pork meat, minced
- 240ml water
- 180g cauliflower, diced small
- 175g cream cheese
- 120ml heavy cream
- 60g shredded cheddar cheese
- Salt, to taste
- 1/4 tsp cayenne pepper
- 1/4 tsp paprika

INSTRUCTIONS:

- Cook the bacon in the air fryer for 4 minutes until crispy at 204°C.
- Boil the cauliflower in hot water for 2 minutes, then drain.
- In a large bowl, mix the boiled cauliflower with the cream cheese, heavy cream, cheddar cheese, salt, pepper, bacon, pork meat, cayenne pepper, and paprika.
- Place the mixture into the air fryer basket and cook for 6 minutes.
- Serve and enjoy.

NUTRITION INFORMATION (PER SERVING):

Calories:	715	
Total Fat:	59.5g	(76% of daily value)
Saturated Fat:	28.1g	(141% of daily value)
Cholesterol:	134mg	(45% of daily value)
Sodium:	2060mg	(90% of daily value)
Total Carbohydrates:	4.7g	(2% of daily value)
Dietary Fiber:	1.1g	(4% of daily value)
Total Sugars:	1.4g	
Protein:	40.1g	

93. Pork Milanese with Stuffed Mushrooms

 Prep: 25 Minutes   **Cook Time:** 37 Minutes   **Serves:** 4

INGREDIENTS:

- 2 eggs, beaten
- 200g seasoned breadcrumbs
- 4 thin-sliced boneless pork chops
- 175g cream cheese
- 125ml sour cream
- 50g baby spinach, chopped
- 1 tsp garlic powder
- Salt and black pepper, to taste
- 5 medium-sized Portobello mushrooms, cored
- 100g Parmesan cheese, grated

INSTRUCTIONS:

- Season the chops with salt and black pepper.
- Put breadcrumbs on a plate.

- Whisk the eggs in a bowl.
- Dip the chops in the eggs, then in the breadcrumbs.
- Add to a greased air fryer basket and cook for 25 minutes at 180°C, flipping halfway through.
- Meanwhile, in a small bowl, mix together the cream cheese, sour cream, garlic powder, salt, pepper, and spinach.
- Fill the mixture into the mushroom cavities and sprinkle with Parmesan cheese.
- Add to the air fryer and cook for 12 minutes at 180°C.
- Serve with the cooked pork chops.

 NUTRITION INFORMATION (PER SERVING):

Calories:	595
Total Fat:	38.6g (49% of daily value)
Saturated Fat:	21.4g (107% of daily value)
Cholesterol:	237mg (79% of daily value)
Sodium:	780mg (34% of daily value)
Total Carbohydrates:	16.6g (6% of daily value)
Dietary Fiber:	1.9g (7% of daily value)
Total Sugars:	0.4g
Protein:	47.9g

94. Pork Bacon and Eggs Pockets

 Prep: 10 Minutes | **Cook Time:** 12 Minutes | **Serves:** 2

INGREDIENTS:

- 6 large pork bacon slices
- 4 organic eggs, whisked
- 115g full-fat cream cheese
- 1 tbsp fresh, chopped chives
- 180-230g whole-wheat pizza dough
- Oil spray, for greasing

INSTRUCTIONS:

- Preheat the air fryer for 3 minutes at 204°C.
- Cook the bacon in a large skillet until crispy and crumble once cooled.
- Cook the eggs in the same skillet until firm.
- In a bowl, mix together the eggs, bacon crumbs, chives, and cream cheese.
- Roll out the pizza dough on a flat surface and cut into 4 equal pieces.

- Divide the mixture between the pieces of pizza dough, brush the edges with water, and wrap the dough around the mixture, sealing the edges.
- Place in a greased air fryer basket.
- Cook for 12 minutes, flipping halfway through.
- Serve hot and enjoy.

 NUTRITION INFORMATION (PER SERVING):

Calories:	832
Total Fat:	53.4g (68% of daily value)
Saturated Fat:	26.1g (130% of daily value)
Cholesterol:	452mg (151% of daily value)
Sodium:	2079mg (90% of daily value)
Total Carbohydrates:	39.5g (14% of daily value)
Dietary Fiber:	6.1g (22% of daily value)
Total Sugars:	5.4g
Protein:	45.6g

95. Air Fryer Roast Pork Belly with Rocket Salad

 Prep: 25 Minutes | **Cook Time:** 25 Minutes | **Serves:** 4

INGREDIENTS:

- 900g boneless pork belly
- Salt and black pepper, to taste
- Oil spray, for greasing

ROCKET SALAD INGREDIENTS:

- 2 bunches of arugula, washed, dried, and torn
- 80ml extra-virgin olive oil
- Juice of 1/3 lemon
- Salt and black pepper, to taste
- 80g of Parmigiano-Reggiano

INSTRUCTIONS:

- Mix all the Rocket salad ingredients in a bowl and set aside.
- Preheat the air fryer for 2 minutes at 200°C.
- Grease the pork with oil and place in the air fryer basket.
- Cook for 15-22 minutes, or until the rind starts to crackle.
- Reduce the temperature to 160°C and cook for a further 25 minutes, or until the pork is tender.
- Season with salt and black pepper and serve with the Rocket salad and a sprinkle of flaky salt.

NUTRITION INFORMATION (PER SERVING):

Calories:	1430	
Total Fat:	146.4g	(188% of daily value)
Saturated Fat:	50.2g	(251% of daily value)
Cholesterol:	139mg	(46% of daily value)
Sodium:	8339mg	(363% of daily value)
Total Carbohydrates:	1.2g	(0% of daily value)
Dietary Fiber:	0.1g	(0% of daily value)
Total Sugars:	0.1g	
Protein:	25g	

96. Garlic Rosemary Pork Chops with Sour Cream

 Prep: 20 Minutes | **Cook Time:** 18 Minutes | **Serves:** 2

INGREDIENTS:

- 2 rosemary leaves
- 1/2 tsp fresh thyme, chopped
- Salt and black pepper, to taste
- 2 garlic cloves
- 110g butter
- 45ml olive oil
- 6 pork chops
- 225g sour cream

INSTRUCTIONS:

- Blend the oil, thyme, rosemary, salt, black pepper, garlic, and butter in a food processor until a paste forms.
- Marinate the pork chops in the paste for 1 hour in the refrigerator.
- Grease the air fryer basket with oil and place the pork chops in the basket.
- Cook for 18 minutes at 200°C, flipping halfway through.
- Serve with a dollop of sour cream.

 NUTRITION INFORMATION (PER SERVING):

Calories:	1403	
Total Fat:	127.8g	(164% of daily value)
Saturated Fat:	54.9g	(275% of daily value)
Cholesterol:	318mg	(106% of daily value)
Sodium:	393mg	(17% of daily value)
Total Carbohydrates:	6.1g	(2% of daily value)
Dietary Fiber:	0.2g	(1% of daily value)
Total Sugars:	0.2g	
Protein:	58g	

97. Saucy Beef Chops

 Prep: 25 Minutes | **Cook Time:** 22 Minutes | **Makes:** 2 Servings

INGREDIENTS:

- Sauce:
- 30g dry mustard powder
- 60g brown sugar, packed
- 60ml bourbon
- 80g ketchup
- 15ml Worcestershire sauce
- 60ml soy sauce
- Salt and pepper, to taste
- Meat:
- 6 beef chops
- Oil spray, for greasing

DIRECTIONS:

- In a large bowl, mix the sauce ingredients well.
- Marinate the beef chops by coating them in the sauce and letting them sit in the refrigerator for 2 hours.
- Add the beef chops to an air fryer basket that has been greased with oil spray.
- Cook for 12 minutes at 400°F (204°C), flipping halfway through.
- Baste the steak with the sauce after halftime has passed.
- Drizzle with sauce once cooked and serve.
- Nutrition Facts:

Servings:	2

Amount per serving:

Calories:	495	
Total Fat:	18.7g	(24% Daily Value)
Saturated Fat:	6.7g	(33% Daily Value)
Cholesterol:	29mg	(10% Daily Value)
Sodium:	3659mg	(159% Daily Value)
Total Carbohydrate:	42.3g	(15% Daily Value)
Dietary Fiber:	3.1g	(11% Daily Value)
Total Sugars:	34.9g	
Protein:	25.4g	

98. Minced Beef and Vegetables Casserole

 Prep: 25 Minutes | **Cook Time:** 25 Minutes | **Makes:** 2 Servings

INGREDIENTS:

- 450g beef, minced
- 80g chopped onion
- 120g green bell pepper, diced

- 225g shredded Cheddar cheese
- 2 eggs, whisked
- Oil spray, for greasing
- Salt and black pepper, to taste
- 120ml almond milk

DIRECTIONS:

- Grease a round air fryer-safe dish with oil spray.
- Layer half of the onion, green pepper, meat, and cheese on the bottom of the dish.
- Repeat to create one more layer.
- In a large bowl, beat the eggs and whisk in the milk, salt, and pepper.
- Pour the egg mixture on top of the casserole.
- Add the casserole to the air fryer and cook for 25 minutes at 390°F (198°C).
- Serve once cooked.

 **NUTRITION FACTS:**

Servings: 2

Amount per serving:

Calories:	870	
Total Fat:	51.9g	(67% Daily Value)
Saturated Fat:	31.3g	(157% Daily Value)
Cholesterol:	426mg	(142% Daily Value)
Sodium:	572mg	(25% Daily Value)
Total Carbohydrate:	8.5g	(3% Daily Value)
Dietary Fiber:	2.1g	(8% Daily Value)
Total Sugars:	4.9g	
Protein:	90.3g	

99. Beef Masala Chops

 Prep: 15 Minutes | **Cook Time:** 30-35 Minutes | **Serves:** 2

INGREDIENTS:

- 900g beef chops
- 5g red chilli powder
- 5g turmeric powder
- 5g garam masala powder
- Salt, to taste
- 5g cumin powder
- 10ml white vinegar
- 10g ginger-garlic paste
- 60ml olive oil
- 240ml beef broth

INSTRUCTIONS:

- Heat the oil in a frying pan.
- Add the ginger-garlic paste and cook until fragrant.
- Add the beef chops and cook until browned and the excess meat juices have evaporated.
- Add the remaining ingredients one by one.

- Cook for approximately 15 minutes while adding the beef broth.
- Once the broth has evaporated, add the meat to the air fryer basket and cook for 8 minutes at 204°C.
- Serve with your preferred dip.

 NUTRITION INFORMATION (PER SERVING):

Energy:	2,471kJ
Total Fat:	44.3g
Saturated Fat:	10.5g
Cholesterol:	147mg
Sodium:	3330mg
Total Carbohydrates:	4.4g
Dietary Fiber:	0.8g
Total Sugars:	0.3g
Protein:	45.4g

100. Air Fryer Beef Kebabs

 Prep: 26 Minutes | **Cook Time:** 22 Minutes | **Serves:** 4

INGREDIENTS:

- 900g beef, trimmed
- 2 ripe mangos
- 1 large red bell pepper

Marinade Ingredients:

- 80ml orange juice
- 60ml honey
- 30ml vegetable oil
- 30g rotisserie seasoning

Salad Ingredients:

- 115g baby arugula
- 2 ripe avocados, cubed
- 2 red onions, thinly sliced
- 240ml canned black beans, drained and rinsed

INSTRUCTIONS:

- Mix the salad ingredients in a bowl and set aside.
- Cut the tenderloin into 16 pieces.
- Mix the marinade ingredients in a large bowl.
- Stir the meat, mango, bell pepper, and marinade together in a large mixing bowl.
- Mix well.
- On each skewer, thread 2 pieces of meat, 2 pieces of mango, and 2 pieces of bell pepper.

- Place the skewers in the air fryer and cook for 6 minutes at 204°C.
- Cook the skewers for an additional 10-12 minutes at 204°C.
- Just before serving, toss the skewers with 2 tablespoons of marinade.
- Drizzle the remaining marinade over the skewers and serve with the salad.

 NUTRITION INFORMATION (PER SERVING):

Energy:	4,501kJ
Total Fat:	42.2g
Saturated Fat:	11.1g
Cholesterol:	203mg
Sodium:	171mg
Total Carbohydrates:	91.9g
Dietary Fiber:	18.9g
Total Sugars:	47.9g
Protein:	84.4g

101. Air Fryer Teriyaki Beef and Pineapple Kabobs

 Prep: 26 Minutes | **Cook Time:** 22 Minutes | **Serves:** 4

INGREDIENTS

- 700g beef, cubed
- 650g pineapple chunks

Teriyaki Sauce Ingredients

- 80ml soy sauce
- 80ml brown sugar
- 4 teaspoons pineapple juice
- 4 teaspoons minced garlic
- 15ml minced ginger
- Slurry for Sauce
- 4 teaspoons cold water
- 4 teaspoons cornstarch

DIRECTIONS

- In a saucepan, simmer all the teriyaki sauce ingredients. Reserve half of the sauce for later use.
- Marinate the beef in the remaining sauce for 30 minutes.
- While the beef is marinating, heat the reserved sauce in the saucepan and add the cornstarch and water mixture. Cook for 5 minutes.
- Thread the wooden skewers with beef cubes and pineapple alternately.
- Mist the skewers with oil spray and add them to the air fryer basket. Cook for 12 minutes at 204°C.

- Serve with the reserved teriyaki sauce.

 NUTRITION FACTS

Servings:		4
Amount per serving:		
Calories:	1064	
Total Fat:	42.2g	(54% of Daily Value)
Saturated Fat:	11.1g	(56% of Daily Value)
Cholesterol:	203mg	(68% of Daily Value)
Sodium:	171mg	(7% of Daily Value)
Total Carbohydrates:	91.9g	(33% of Daily Value)
Dietary Fiber:	18.9g	(67% of Daily Value)
Total Sugars:	47.9g	
Protein:	84.4g	

102. Easy Air Fryer Steak Bites

 Prep: 12 Minutes | **Cook Time:** 9 Minutes | **Serves:** 2

INGREDIENTS

- 450g sirloin steak, cut into bite-sized pieces
- 15ml steak seasoning
- Salt and pepper, to taste
- Olive oil, as needed

DIRECTIONS

- Preheat the air fryer to 204°C.
- In a bowl, combine the steak bites, steak seasoning, salt, and pepper.
- Toss with a tablespoon of olive oil and coat the steak bites completely.
- Arrange the steak bites in a single layer in the air fryer basket and cook for 5 minutes.
- Flip the steak bites and cook for another 4 minutes.
- Remove from the air fryer and set aside for 7 minutes to allow the meat to absorb the juices.
- Serve.

 NUTRITION FACTS

Servings:		2
Amount per serving:		
Calories:	481	
Total Fat:	21.1g	(27% of Daily Value)
Saturated Fat:	6.3g	(32% of Daily Value)
Cholesterol:	203mg	(68% of Daily Value)
Sodium:	149mg	(6% of Daily Value)
Total Carbohydrates:	0g	(0% of Daily Value)
Dietary Fiber:	0g	(0% of Daily Value)
Total Sugars:	0g	
Protein:	68.8g	

103. Juicy Vegetables and Sirloin Steak with Sour Cream

 Prep: 12 Minutes | **Cook Time:** 12 Minutes | **Serves:** 3

INGREDIENTS:

- 680g beef sirloin steak, cut into strips
- 60ml beef broth
- 125g diced tomatoes, un-drained
- 170g green beans, halved
- 170g frozen pearl onions, thawed
- 1 tbsp paprika
- 250ml sour cream
- Oil spray, for greasing
- Salt and black pepper, to taste

DIRECTIONS:

- Preheat the air fryer to 204ºC.
- In a large bowl, combine the steak strips, broth, green beans, tomatoes, onions, paprika, salt, and black pepper.
- Grease the air fryer basket with oil spray and add the steak mixture to the basket.
- Cook for 12 minutes, then set aside for 5-10 minutes to allow the meat to absorb the juices.
- Serve with a dollop of sour cream.

NUTRITION FACTS (PER SERVING):

Calories:	620	
Fat:	30.9g	(40% of daily value)
Saturated Fat:	15.5g	(77% of daily value)
Cholesterol:	236mg	(79% of daily value)
Sodium:	259mg	(11% of daily value)
Carbohydrates:	9.9g	(4% of daily value)
Fiber:	3.2g	(11% of daily value)
Sugars:	2g	
Protein:	73.3g	

104. Italian-Style Beef Meatballs

 Prep: 26 Minutes | **Cook Time:** 12 Minutes | **Serves:** 2

INGREDIENTS:

- 2 tbsp olive oil
- 2 medium shallots, minced
- 2 cloves garlic, minced
- 125g Panko breadcrumbs
- 150ml whole milk
- 585g lean ground beef
- 450g bulk turkey sausage
- 2 large eggs, lightly beaten
- 60g fresh flat-leaf parsley, chopped
- 2 tbsp rosemary, chopped
- 1 tbsp thyme, chopped
- 2 tbsp Dijon mustard

DIRECTIONS:

- Preheat the air fryer to 204ºC.
- In a skillet, heat the oil and cook the shallots for 2 minutes. Then, add the garlic and cook for 2 minutes.
- In a separate bowl, combine the Panko breadcrumbs and milk. Then, add the ground beef, turkey sausage, eggs, parsley, rosemary, thyme, mustard, shallot and garlic mixture, and salt.
- Gently mix the ingredients and form meatballs, approximately 3.8cm in diameter.
- Place the meatballs in the air fryer basket and cook for 12 minutes or until lightly browned.
- Serve.

NUTRITION FACTS (PER SERVING):

Calories:	1540	
Fat:	103g	(132% of daily value)
Saturated Fat:	31.5g	(158% of daily value)
Cholesterol:	640mg	(213% of daily value)
Sodium:	2147mg	(93% of daily value)
Carbohydrates:	5.7g	(2% of daily value)
Fiber:	2.7g	(10% of daily value)
Sugars:	0.6g	
Protein:	141.2g	

105. Beef Stuffed Bell Peppers

 Prep: 20 Minutes | **Cook Time:** 20 Minutes | **Serves:** 2

INGREDIENTS:

- 4 large bell peppers
- 250g cooked rice
- 250g cooked minced beef
- 100g Parmesan cheese
- Salt and black pepper, to taste
- 1 teaspoon cayenne pepper
- 1/2 teaspoon paprika
- Oil spray, for greasing

DIRECTIONS:

- Preheat the air fryer to 204ºC for 2 minutes.
- Cut the tops off the bell peppers and remove all seeds from the center.

- Mix together the remaining ingredients in a bowl and fill the bell peppers with the mixture.
- Place the peppers in the air fryer basket and cook for 20 minutes at 204°C.
- Serve hot.

 NUTRITION FACTS:

Servings:	2	

Per serving:

Energy:	466 kcal	
Fat:	41g	(53% of daily value)
Saturated Fat:	21.2g	(106% of daily value)
Cholesterol:	336mg	(112% of daily value)
Sodium:	1115mg	(48% of daily value)
Carbohydrates:	59.3g	(22% of daily value)
Dietary Fiber:	4.3g	(15% of daily value)
Sugars:	12.2g	
Protein:	127.8g	

106. Spicy Beef Fillet

 Prep: 10 Minutes | **Cook Time:** 16 Minutes | **Serves:** 1

INGREDIENTS:

- 400g beef fillet
- Salt and black pepper, to taste
- 15g butter, melted
- 1/2 teaspoon lemon juice
- 1/2 teaspoon chopped rosemary
- 1/2 teaspoon chopped thyme
- Oil spray, for greasing

DIRECTIONS:

- Rub the beef fillet with salt, lemon juice, thyme, rosemary, and black pepper.
- Place the fillet in the air fryer and cook for 8 minutes on each side at 204°C.
- Brush the fillet with melted butter before serving.
- Allow the fillet to rest for 5-10 minutes before serving.

 NUTRITION FACTS:

Servings:	1	

Per serving:

Energy:	466 kcal	
Fat:	52.2g	(67% of daily value)
Saturated Fat:	23.5g	(117% of daily value)
Cholesterol:	391mg	(130% of daily value)
Sodium:	4083mg	(178% of daily value)
Carbohydrates:	16.9g	(6% of daily value)
Dietary Fiber:	0.5g	(2% of daily value)

Sugars:	16.1g
Protein:	144.2g

107. Coconut Lamb Chops

 Prep: 12 Minutes | **Cook Time:** 22 Minutes | **Serves:** 2

INGREDIENTS

- Oil spray, for greasing
- 6 lamb chops
- Sauce ingredients
- Salt and ground black pepper, to taste
- 2 tablespoons butter, for frying
- 1 1/2 teaspoons red curry paste
- 280g of coconut cream
- 2 tablespoons fresh coriander, chopped
- 3 green chillies, finely chopped

DIRECTIONS

- Preheat the air fryer to 204°C for 2 minutes.
- In a large bowl, mix all the sauce ingredients.
- Combine well and let the chops marinate in the mixture for 2 hours in the refrigerator.
- Cook the chops in the air fryer basket for 22 minutes at 204°C.
- Once done, serve.

 NUTRITION FACTS

Servings:	2	

Amount per serving

Calories	2220	

% Daily Value*

Total Fat	113.5g	145%
Saturated Fat	58.8g	294%
Cholesterol	913mg	304%
Sodium	1041mg	45%
Total Carbohydrate	7.5g	3%
Dietary Fiber	2.7g	10%
Total Sugars	4g	
Protein	278.4g	

108. Lamb Meat Roll-Ups

 Prep: 15 Minutes | **Cook Time:** 12 Minutes | **Serves:** 2

INGREDIENTS

- 2 packs of refrigerated crescent rolls

- 10 slices of smoked lamb meat
- 4 slices of Swiss cheese
- 225g of Sauerkraut
- 1 tablespoon bagel seasoning, as needed
- Oil spray, for greasing

DIRECTIONS

- Preheat the air fryer to 204°C for 2 minutes.
- On a clean work surface, lay out the crescent roll dough and separate into 10 rectangles.
- Cut the cheese into small slices and distribute it evenly among the rectangle shapes.
- Add equal portions of meat, seasoning, and sauerkraut.
- Roll up the dough and pinch the edges.
- Cut the rolls in half and grease with oil spray.
- Cook in an air fryer basket lined with parchment paper for 12 minutes at 204°C.
- Once cooked, serve and enjoy.

NUTRITION FACTS

Servings: 2

Amount per serving
Calories 1487

% Daily Value*

Total Fat	97g	124%
Saturated Fat	47.5g	238%
Cholesterol	452mg	151%
Sodium	1477mg	64%
Total Carbohydrate	18.9g	7%
Dietary Fiber	3.3g	12%
Total Sugars	4.8g	
Protein	122.1g	

109. Hearty Lamb Chops Tomatina

 Prep: 15 Minutes | **Cook Time:** 12 Minutes | **Serves:** 2

INGREDIENTS:

- 6 boneless and cubed lamb chops (about 680g)
- 25g fresh basil leaves
- 4 plum tomatoes (about 400g)
- 185ml vinegar
- 30ml olive oil
- 2 minced garlic cloves
- Salt and pepper, to taste

DIRECTIONS:

- Blend together all ingredients, except the lamb chops, in a blender.
- Marinate the lamb chops in the blended mixture and refrigerate for 1 hour.
- Preheat the air fryer to 204°C.
- Cook the marinated lamb chops in the air fryer for 12 minutes, flipping halfway through.
- Serve hot.

NUTRITION FACTS:

Servings: 2

Per serving:

Calories	2025	
Total Fat	86.4g	(111%)
Saturated Fat	27.8g	(139%)
Cholesterol	883mg	(294%)
Sodium	783mg	(34%)
Total Carbohydrates	14.5g	(5%)
Dietary Fiber	2.8g	(10%)
Total Sugars	10.2g	
Protein	278.7g	

110. Pesto Steak and Pasta

 Prep: 20 Minutes | **Cook Time:** 30 Minutes | **Serves:** 4

INGREDIENTS:

- Salt and pepper, to taste
- 100g feta cheese, crumbled
- 60g pesto, prepared and homemade
- 50g walnuts, chopped
- 225g grape tomatoes, halved
- 225g penne pasta, uncooked
- 175g baby spinach, chopped
- 2 lamb steaks

DIRECTIONS:

- Cook the pasta according to package instructions, then drain and set aside.
- Season the lamb steaks with salt, pepper, and oil.
- Preheat the air fryer to 204°C.
- Cook the lamb steaks in the air fryer for 12 minutes, flipping halfway through.
- In a large bowl, mix together the cooked pasta, walnuts, spinach, tomatoes, and pesto sauce.
- Top with the cooked lamb steaks and sprinkle with feta cheese.
- Serve and enjoy.

NUTRITION FACTS:

Servings:	4	

Per serving:

Calories	1138	
Total Fat	40.4g	(52%)
Saturated Fat	12.3g	(62%)
Cholesterol	324mg	(108%)
Sodium	724mg	(31%)
Total Carbohydrates	112.5g	(41%)
Dietary Fiber	2.8g	(10%)
Total Sugars	4.1g	
Protein	79.8g	

111. Rolled Empanadas

 Prep:
30 Minutes

 Cook Time:
25 Minutes

 Makes:
4 Servings

INGREDIENTS

- 450g minced lamb meat
- 450g puff pastry
- 2 tbsp olive oil
- 2 green peppers, diced
- 1 onion, peeled and chopped
- 2 garlic cloves, peeled and chopped
- 1/2 tsp cumin
- 225g tomato sauce
- Sea salt and pepper to taste
- 2 egg yolks
- 4 tbsp full-fat milk

DIRECTIONS

- Heat the oil in a skillet and cook the minced lamb meat for 10 minutes.
- Drain any liquid, add the garlic and cook until fragrant.
- Add all the ingredients except the pastry, milk, and egg yolks. Cook the mixture for another 10 minutes.
- In a separate bowl, whisk the egg yolks and milk together to create a binding agent.
- Roll out the puff pastry on a flat surface.
- Let the cooked mixture cool and add it to the pastry.
- Roll the pastry to seal the edges and brush with the egg wash. Repeat until all the pastries are done.
- Cook the pastries in an air fryer for 14 minutes at 400°F (204°C), flipping them halfway through.
- Serve hot.

 NUTRITION FACTS

Servings:	4	

Amount per serving

Calories	1142	

% Daily Value*

Total Fat	71.8g	92%
Saturated Fat	20g	100%
Cholesterol	221mg	74%
Sodium	1519mg	66%
Total Carbohydrate	76.8g	28%
Dietary Fiber	7.4g	26%
Total Sugars	10.3g	
Protein	44g	

112. Loin Lamb Chops

 Prep:
12 Minutes

Cook Time:
16 Minutes

 Makes:
2 Servings

INGREDIENTS

- 3 garlic cloves, sliced
- 2 tbsp minced rosemary leaves
- 2 tsp red wine vinegar
- 2 tbsp soy sauce
- 2 tbsp olive oil
- 4-5 loin lamb chops, 1 ½ in. thick

DIRECTIONS

- Mix all the ingredients in a bowl excluding the lamb chops.
- Marinate the chops in the mixture for 1 hour.
- Grease the air fryer basket with oil spray.
- Cook the lamb chops in the air fryer for 16 minutes at 350°F (176°C), flipping halfway through.
- Serve hot.

 NUTRITION FACTS

Servings:	2	

Amount per serving

Calories	1191	

% Daily Value*

Total Fat	99.3g	127%
Saturated Fat	38.1g	191%
Cholesterol	261mg	87%
Sodium	1117mg	49%
Total Carbohydrate	4.9g	2%
Dietary Fiber	1.6g	6%
Total Sugars	0.3g	
Protein	63.4g	

113. Mojito Spiced Ribs

 Prep:
20 Minutes

 Cook Time:
14 Minutes

 Makes:
2 Servings

INGREDIENTS:

- 60 ml lemon juice (from 2 lemons)
- 60 ml olive oil
- 20 g fresh mint, chopped
- 4 large garlic cloves, minced
- 4-6 lamb rib chops, trimmed
- Salt, to taste

DIRECTIONS:

- Combine the lemon juice, salt, oil, mint leaves, and garlic in a blender. Pulse until smooth.
- Coat the lamb chops with the mixture and let it marinate in the refrigerator for 30 minutes.
- Place the lamb chops in the air fryer basket.
- Cook for 14 minutes at 400 degrees F (204 degrees C), flipping halfway through.
- Serve hot.

 NUTRITION FACTS:

Servings: 2

Amount per serving:

Calories:	1432	
Total Fat:	73.1 g	(94%)
Saturated Fat:	20.7 g	(104%)
Cholesterol:	589 mg	(196%)
Sodium:	575 mg	(25%)
Total Carbohydrate:	0 g	(0%)
Dietary Fiber:	0 g	(0%)
Total Sugars:	0 g	
Protein:	183.6 g	

114. Lamb Sandwich

 Prep:
10 Minutes

 Cook Time:
25-28 Minutes

 Makes:
4 Servings

INGREDIENTS:

- 12 strips of bacon
- 4 slices of white bread
- 60 ml ranch dressing
- 450 g cooked lamb meat
- 4 slices of Parmesan cheese
- 2 teaspoons salted butter

DIRECTIONS:

- Add the bacon strips to the air fryer basket and cook for 12 minutes at 400 degrees F (204 degrees C) until crisp. Set aside.
- Butter the two slices of bread and cook in the air fryer basket, butter side down.
- Layer the bread slices with ranch dressing, shredded lamb meat, cooked bacon slices, and Parmesan cheese.
- Top with the remaining bread slices to make sandwiches.
- Cook for 14 minutes at 400 degrees F (204 degrees C), flipping halfway through.
- Serve and enjoy.

 NUTRITION FACTS:

Servings: 4

Amount per serving:

Calories:	622	
Total Fat:	41.8 g	(54%)
Saturated Fat:	17.4 g	(87%)
Cholesterol:	138 mg	(46%)
Sodium:	1166 mg	(51%)
Total Carbohydrate:	12.4 g	(4%)
Dietary Fiber:	3.3 g	(12%)
Total Sugars:	0.8 g	
Protein:	47.9 g	

115. Mint and Greek Yogurt Chops

 Prep:
15 Minutes

Cook Time:
22 Minutes

 Makes:
4 Servings

INGREDIENTS:

- 60 ml lemon juice
- 240 g Greek yogurt
- 60 g parsley, chopped
- 120 g mint, chopped
- 5 g five-spice powder
- Salt and black pepper, to taste
- 2.5 g ginger garlic paste
- 8 lamb chops
- Oil spray, for greasing

DIRECTIONS:

- Pulse all the ingredients except the lamb chops in a blender and make a smooth paste.
- Marinate the chops in the mixture for a few hours in the refrigerator.

- Put the chops in the air fryer basket and cook for 16 minutes at 176°C, flipping halfway through.
- Once cooked, serve hot.

 NUTRITION FACTS:

Servings:	4	
Amount per serving:		
Calories	- 2527	
Total Fat	- 98.5g	(126%)
Saturated Fat	- 36g	(180%)
Cholesterol	- 1182mg	(394%)
Sodium	- 1041mg	(45%)
Total Carbohydrate	- 6.7g	(2%)
Dietary Fiber	- 1.9g	(7%)
Total Sugars	- 4.4g	
Protein	- 378.4g	

116. Raspberry Chipotle Lamb Chop

 Prep: 20 Minutes | **Cook Time:** 18 Minutes | **Makes:** 4 Servings

INGREDIENTS:

- 6 lamb chops
- 480 g fresh homemade coleslaw
- 240 g cheese sauce

Sauce Ingredients:

- 20 g chipotle seasoning
- 120 ml coconut amino
- 120 ml raspberry sauce
- 30 ml honey
- 2.5 g garlic powder
- Salt, to taste
- 2.5 g paprika powder

DIRECTIONS:

- Whisk all the sauce ingredients in a bowl.
- Marinate the chops in the sauce for 1 hour in the refrigerator.
- Cook the chops in an air fryer basket greased with oil spray for 12 minutes at 204°C, flipping halfway through.
- Simmer the leftover sauce in a skillet and cook for 5 minutes until reduced.
- Serve hot with coleslaw and cheese sauce.

 NUTRITION FACTS:

Servings:	4	
Amount per serving:		
Calories	- 1673	
Total Fat	- 93.3g	(120%)
Saturated Fat	- 26.2g	(131%)
Cholesterol	- 528mg	(176%)
Sodium	- 2363mg	(103%)
Total Carbohydrate	- 56.4g	(20%)
Dietary Fiber	- 0.3g	(1%)
Total Sugars	- 49.2g	
Protein	- 147.7g	

07 | **Seafood**
Recipes

117. Shrimp Omelet With Mushroom In Air Fryer

 Prep:
15 Minutes

 Cook Time:
12 Minutes

 Makes:
2 Servings

INGREDIENTS:

- 2 large eggs
- 1 small onion, diced
- 15 g butter
- 60 ml almond milk
- 60 g grated cheese
- 120 g chopped shrimps
- 120 g chopped mushrooms
- Salt, to taste
- Black pepper, to taste

DIRECTIONS:

- In a mixing bowl, beat the eggs, add the butter, and almond milk and mix well.
- Add the grated cheese to the mixture.
- Add salt, pepper, and the diced onion, as well as the chopped shrimps and mushrooms.
- Preheat the air fryer to 180°C (356°F).
- Pour the mixture into two greased ramekins.
- Place the ramekins in the air fryer basket and cook for 12 minutes at 180°C (356°F).
- Once done, remove from the air fryer and serve.

NUTRITION FACTS (PER SERVING):

Calories:	284	
Total Fat:	22.4 g	(29%)
Saturated Fat:	14.4 g	(72%)
Cholesterol:	240 mg	(80%)
Sodium:	328 mg	(14%)
Total Carbohydrates:	6.4 g	(2%)
Dietary Fiber:	1.6 g	(6%)
Total Sugars:	3.2 g	
Protein:	15.8 g	

118. Shrimp, Mushroom, and Broccoli

 Prep:
15 Minutes

 Cook Time:
8 Minutes

 Makes:
1 Serving

INGREDIENTS:

- 450 g shrimp
- 3 cloves of garlic, chopped
- 125 g broccoli florets
- 15 ml soy sauce
- 2.5 g stevia
- Cooking oil spray
- 15 ml lemon juice
- 115 g shiitake mushrooms, chopped

DIRECTIONS:

- Preheat the air fryer to 180°C (356°F) for 5 minutes.
- In a mixing bowl, add the chopped garlic, soy sauce, and stevia.
- Add the shrimps to the bowl and mix well.
- Add the broccoli, lemon juice, and mushrooms to the shrimp mixture.
- Spray the air fryer basket with cooking oil.
- Add the shrimp mixture to the air fryer basket and cook for 8 minutes at 180°C (356°F).
- Once done, remove from the air fryer and serve.

NUTRITION FACTS (PER SERVING):

Calories:	641	
Total Fat:	8.3 g	(11%)
Saturated Fat:	2.5 g	(13%)
Cholesterol:	955 mg	(318%)
Sodium:	2300 mg	(100%)
Total Carbohydrates:	30.1 g	(11%)
Dietary Fiber:	3.9 g	(14%)
Total Sugars:	5.5 g	
Protein:	108 g	

119. Shrimp and Cauliflower

 Prep: 10 Minutes | **Cook Time:** 8 Minutes | **Makes:** 2 Servings

INGREDIENTS:

- 450g shrimp
- 3 cloves garlic, chopped
- 225g cauliflower
- 20ml oyster sauce
- 5g brown sugar
- Cooking oil spray
- 15ml lemon juice

DIRECTIONS:

- Preheat the air fryer to 350ºF (176ºC) for 5 minutes.
- In a mixing bowl, combine the garlic, oyster sauce, and sugar.
- Add the shrimp to the bowl and mix well.
- Add the cauliflower and lemon juice to the shrimp mixture.
- Spray the air fryer basket with cooking oil and place the shrimp mixture in it.
- Cook for 8 minutes.
- Serve once cooked.

 NUTRITION FACTS (PER SERVING):

Calories:	321	
Fat:	4.1g	(5% of daily value)
Saturated Fat:	1.3g	(6%)
Cholesterol:	478mg	(159%)
Sodium:	1150mg	(50%)
Total Carbohydrates:	15g	(5%)
Dietary Fiber:	2g	(7%)
Total Sugars:	2.8g	
Protein:	54g	

120. Salmon Cake

 Prep: 15 Minutes | **Cook Time:** 20 Minutes | **Makes:** 1 Serving

INGREDIENTS:

- 140g pink salmon
- 1 medium-sized egg
- 60g Panko breadcrumbs
- 1 tablespoon fresh dill, chopped
- 1 tablespoon mayonnaise
- 1 teaspoon Dijon mustard
- 2 lemon wedges, sliced
- Salt and black pepper, to taste
- Cooking spray

DIRECTIONS:

- Preheat the air fryer to 390ºF (199ºC) for 12 minutes.
- Remove the bones and skin from the salmon and place it in a mixing bowl.
- In the mixing bowl, whisk together the egg, salmon, dill, mustard, pepper, and mayonnaise.
- Shape the mixture into small patties.
- Coat the patties with cooking spray.
- Coat both sides of the patties with Panko breadcrumbs.
- Place the patties in the air fryer basket and cook for 6 minutes, flipping halfway through.
- Serve once cooked.

 NUTRITION FACTS (PER SERVING):

Calories:	300	
Fat:	14.8g	(19% of daily value)
Saturated Fat:	2.1g	(10%)
Cholesterol:	66mg	(22%)
Sodium:	298mg	(13%)
Total Carbohydrates:	10.9g	(4%)
Dietary Fiber:	1.5g	(5%)
Total Sugars:	1.7g	
Protein:	32.7g	

121. Coconut Shrimp

 Prep: 15 Minutes | **Cook Time:** 14 Minutes | **Serves:** 1

INGREDIENTS:

- 5 large shrimps, cleaned
- 50g unsweetened coconut, dried
- 50g Panko breadcrumbs
- 1 large egg
- 1 teaspoon cornstarch
- 50g flour

INSTRUCTIONS:

- Preheat the air fryer to 160ºC.
- Thoroughly wash the shrimps and place them on a paper towel to dry.
- Whisk the egg in a bowl and set aside.
- Mix the coconut flakes and breadcrumbs on a baking sheet.
- In a separate bowl, mix the flour and cornstarch.
- Dip each shrimp in the flour mixture, then in the egg, and finally in the coconut mixture.
- Place the shrimps in the air fryer basket.
- Cook for 14 minutes at 160ºC.
- Serve hot.

NUTRITION INFORMATION:

Servings:	1

Amount per serving:
Calories:	776
Fat:	24.6g (31% of daily value)
Saturated Fat:	15.6g (78% of daily value)
Cholesterol:	418mg (139% of daily value)
Sodium:	348mg (15% of daily value)
Carbohydrates:	66.5g (24% of daily value)
Fiber:	5.5g (20% of daily value)
Sugar:	3.1g
Protein:	40.6g

122. Fish Sandwich

 Prep: 15 Minutes   **Cook Time:** 20 Minutes **Serves:** 2

INGREDIENTS:

- 450g white fish fillet
- 2 toasted buns
- 1 tablespoon mayonnaise
- 50g Panko breadcrumbs
- 1 tablespoon Cajun seasoning
- Salt, pinch

Lemon Mayo Ingredients:

- 60g mayonnaise
- 1 teaspoon lemon zest
- 1 tablespoon Dijon mustard
- 1 tablespoon lemon juice
- 1 tablespoon dill relish
- Toppings:
- 2 sliced tomatoes
- 2 leaves of lettuce or arugula
- A few pickles

INSTRUCTIONS:

- Preheat the air fryer to 220°C.
- Mix all the ingredients for the lemon mayo in a bowl and set aside.
- Season each fish fillet with Cajun seasoning and a pinch of salt.
- Apply mayonnaise to each fillet.
- Dip each fillet in the Panko breadcrumbs.
- Place the fish fillets in the air fryer basket.
- Cook for 20 minutes at 220°C.
- Once the fish is cooked, place it on a toasted bun, add the toppings, and spread the lemon mayo on the other bun.
- Serve hot.

 NUTRITION INFORMATION:

Servings:	2

Amount per serving:
Calories:	655
Fat:	29.7g (38% of daily value)
Saturated Fat:	4.6g (23% of daily value)
Cholesterol:	186mg (62% of daily value)
Sodium:	873mg (38% of daily value)
Carbohydrates:	32.2g (12% of daily value)
Fiber:	2.3g (8% of daily value)
Sugar:	7.2g
Protein:	61g

123. Fish Cakes

 Prep: 15 Minutes   **Cook Time:** 15 Minutes **Makes:** 2 Servings

INGREDIENTS:

- 227g mashed potatoes
- 227g white fish
- 1 small onion, chopped
- 5g butter
- 10ml milk
- 1 tsp lime zest
- 2 tsp chili powder
- 1 tsp Worcestershire sauce
- 1 tsp coriander powder
- 1 tsp mixed spice
- 1 tsp mixed herbs
- 50g breadcrumbs from wholemeal bread
- Salt and pepper to taste

DIRECTIONS:

- Place the fish in a pan with the milk and cook until the fish is tender.
- Drain the fish and place it in a mixing bowl.
- Mix the mashed potatoes with the spices in the bowl. The mixture should not form any lumps.
- Add the butter and the remaining ingredients to the bowl and mix well.
- Chill the mixture in the refrigerator for 3 hours to allow the fish to coat well.
- Preheat the air fryer to 200°C.
- Place spoonfuls of the fish mixture into the air fryer and cook for 15 minutes.
- Serve the cooked fish cakes hot.

 NUTRITION FACTS (PER SERVING):

Calories:	203
Total Fat:	5.8g (7% of daily value)
Saturated Fat:	2.3g (12% of daily value)
Cholesterol:	43mg (14% of daily value)
Sodium:	532mg (23% of daily value)

Total Carbohydrates:	15.1g	(5% of daily value)
Dietary Fiber:	1.9g	(7% of daily value)
Total Sugars:	2g	
Protein:	22.7g	

124. Tandoori Fish Tikka

Prep: 15 Minutes	**Cook Time:** 10 Minutes	**Makes:** 2 Servings

INGREDIENTS:

- 2 fish fillets of Mahi-Mahi
- 1/2 rainbow pepper, sliced
- 1 medium-sized onion, sliced
- For Tandoori Marinate:
- 30ml light olive oil
- 30g plain yogurt
- 1 tsp crushed ginger
- 1 tsp crushed garlic
- 15ml lime juice
- 5g salt
- 1/4 tsp turmeric
- 1 tsp ground coriander
- 1/2 tsp cumin powder
- 1 tsp garam masala
- 1 tsp Kashmir red chili powder or paprika
- 1/2 tsp cayenne
- 1 tsp dry fenugreek leaves

DIRECTIONS:

- In a mixing bowl, combine all the ingredients for the tandoori marinate.
- Marinate the fish fillets, rainbow pepper, and onion in the mixture.
- Place the marinated fish, onions, and peppers in the air fryer basket.
- Preheat the air fryer to 360°C and cook for 8-10 minutes.
- Serve the cooked Tandoori Fish Tikka hot.

 NUTRITION FACTS (PER SERVING):

Calories:	216	
Total Fat:	17.4g	(22% of daily value)
Saturated Fat:	2.9g	(14% of daily value)
Cholesterol:	9mg	(3% of daily value)
Sodium:	1301mg	(57% of daily value)
Total Carbohydrates:	11.8g	(4% of daily value)
Dietary Fiber:	2g	(7% of daily value)
Total Sugars		

125. Fish Pakora

Prep: 15 Minutes	**Cook Time:** 13 Minutes	**Makes:** 2 Servings

INGREDIENTS

- 4 fish fillets (180g)
- 1 tsp cumin seeds (2g)
- 1/2 tsp turmeric powder (1g)
- 2 tsp red chili powder (6g)
- 1 tbsp ginger garlic paste (15g)
- 2 tsp rice or tapioca flour (12g)
- 2 tsp gram flour (12g)
- 1 tbsp lemon juice (15ml)
- 2 tsp olive oil (10ml)

DIRECTIONS

- Cut the fish fillet into cubes and wash the fish in the water.
- Add red chili powder, turmeric powder, salt, ginger-garlic paste, rice flour, gram flour, lemon juice, cumin seeds, and a teaspoon of olive oil to the fish fillet cubes.
- Combine everything and marinate the fish with a thickly coated masala.
- Keep the fish in the refrigerator for 30 minutes to an hour.
- Preheat the air fryer to 200°C for 5 minutes.
- Now take the fish from the refrigerator and cook it for 8 minutes.
- Delicious fish pakoras are now ready to serve.

 NUTRITION FACTS

Servings:	2

Amount per serving

Calories:	500
Total Fat:	28g
Saturated Fat:	6g
Cholesterol:	62mg
Sodium:	999mg
Total Carbohydrate:	37.5g
Dietary Fiber:	2.3g
Total Sugars:	0.6g
Protein:	28g

126. Air Fried Tilapia

Prep: 15 Minutes	**Cook Time:** 12 Minutes	**Makes:** 2 Servings

INGREDIENTS

- 2 tilapia fillets (180g)
- 1 tbsp olive oil (15ml)
- 1/4 tsp paprika powder (0.5g)
- 1/4 tsp black pepper powder (0.5g)
- 1 egg

- 1/4 cup all-purpose flour (35g)
- 1/4 cup breadcrumbs (30g)
- Salt, to taste

DIRECTIONS

- Clean, drain the fish and apply olive oil on both sides.
- Preheat the air fryer to 180°C for 3-4 minutes.
- Add paprika powder, salt, and black peppercorn powder to the fish.
- Rub the fish with the all-purpose flour.
- Dip the coated fish in the whisked egg mixture.
- Finally, coat the fillets of fish in breadcrumbs and keep it aside.
- Place the fish fillet in the air fryer. And spray olive oil on the fish fillets.
- Cook the fish fillets in the air fryer for 6 minutes per side.
- Once the fish is cooked, hot crispy fish tilapia is now ready.
- Serve fish tilapia with ketchup, sauce, or a dip.

 NUTRITION FACTS

Servings:	2
Amount per serving	
Calories:	760
Total Fat:	16.2g
Saturated Fat:	4.6g
Cholesterol:	412mg
Sodium:	447mg
Total Carbohydrate:	21.8g
Dietary Fiber:	1g
Total Sugars:	1.1g
Protein:	132.3g

127. Fish Fry

 Prep: 15 Minutes | **Cook Time:** 15 Minutes | **Makes:** 2 Servings

INGREDIENTS:

- Oil for greasing
- 450g fish, fillets
- For Marinate:
- 1 onion or shallot
- 30ml red chili powder
- 2.5g turmeric powder
- Salt to taste
- Water, as needed

DIRECTIONS:

- In a mixing bowl, add the onion or shallot, red chili powder, turmeric powder, salt, and enough water to form a marinade.

- Clean the fish fillets and coat them with the marinade mixture.
- Grease both sides of the fish fillets with oil.
- Place the fish fillets in the air fryer basket and cook for 15 minutes at 190°C.
- Serve the delicious fish fry hot.

 NUTRITION FACTS

Servings:	2	
Amount per serving:		
Calories:	574	
Total Fat:	29.2g	(37%)
Saturated Fat:	6.6g	(33%)
Cholesterol:	77mg	(26%)
Sodium:	1285mg	(56%)
Total Carbohydrate:	48.1g	(17%)
Dietary Fiber:	5g	(18%)
Total Sugars:	2.9g	
Protein:	34.8g	

128. Shrimp Lettuce Wrap

 Prep: 15 Minutes | **Cook Time:** 10 Minutes | **Makes:** 2 Servings

INGREDIENTS:

- 450g shrimp
- 60ml olive oil
- 60ml red wine vinegar
- 2 garlic cloves, finely chopped
- 15ml Italian seasoning
- 15ml lemon juice
- 15ml soy sauce
- 5ml Dijon mustard
- 15ml Worcestershire sauce
- 2 lettuce leaves
- Salt to taste
- Pepper to taste

DIRECTIONS:

- In a mixing bowl, add the red wine vinegar, chopped garlic cloves, olive oil, salt, pepper, lemon juice, Italian seasoning, and soy sauce.
- Add the Worcestershire sauce and mustard to the mixture.
- Add the shrimp to the marinade and refrigerate for 2 hours.
- After 2 hours, take the shrimp out and place them in the air fryer basket.
- Air fry the shrimp at 200°C for 10 minutes.
- Serve the shrimp with lettuce wraps.

NUTRITION FACTS

Servings:	2	
Amount per serving:		
Calories:	534	
Total Fat:	31.3g	(40%)
Saturated Fat:	5.2g	(26%)
Cholesterol:	483mg	(161%)
Sodium:	1199mg	(52%)
Total Carbohydrate:	8.1g	(3%)
Dietary Fiber:	0.3g	(1%)
Total Sugars:	2.6g	
Protein:	52.6g	

129. Sundried Tomato Salmon

 Prep: 15 Minutes | **Cook Time:** 12 Minutes | **Makes:** 1 Serving

INGREDIENTS

- 110g raw salmon
- 25g fresh parsley, chopped
- 15ml Sun-Dried Tomato Dressing
- Oil for greasing
- Required salt
- Black pepper to taste
- 2 Cherry tomatoes
- 125g broccoli

DIRECTIONS

- Preheat the air fryer to 180°C.
- Prepare a bowl with parsley, dressing, salt, and pepper.
- Spray the fish with oil spray and add the above mixture to the fish.
- Place the salmon fillets with the veggies in the air fryer basket.
- Set it to AIRFRY mode for 12 minutes at 200°C.
- Serve the yummy fish once it is cooked.

 NUTRITION FACTS

Servings:	1	
Amount per serving		
Calories	215	
% Daily Value*		
Total Fat	7.8g	10%
Saturated Fat	1.1g	5%
Cholesterol	50mg	17%
Sodium	85mg	4%
Total Carbohydrate	13.6g	5%
Dietary Fiber	4.7g	17%
Total Sugars	7.4g	
Protein	25.9g	

130. Salmon With Dill Dressing

 Prep: 15 Minutes | **Cook Time:** 18 Minutes | **Makes:** 2 Servings

INGREDIENTS

- 2 Salmon fillets
- 2 teaspoons fresh dill
- Salt , to taste
- Black pepper to taste
- For Dill Sauce,
- 60ml low fat plain Greek yogurt
- 2 teaspoons Dijon mustard
- 5ml lemon juice
- 15g chopped fresh dill

DIRECTIONS

- Take a mixing bowl to add all the ingredients for dill sauce and mix it well.
- Place the salmon fillet on a foil sheet.
- Now season the fish with dill, salt, and pepper.
- Seal the Salmon fillet by wrapping the foil.
- Cook the fish for 18 minutes in an air fryer basket at 175°C.
- Air fried Salmon is now ready to eat.
- Serve the fish with Dill sauce and enjoy.

 NUTRITION FACTS

Servings:	2	
Amount per serving		
Calories	261	
% Daily Value*		
Total Fat	11.8g	15%
Saturated Fat	2g	10%
Cholesterol	80mg	27%
Sodium	224mg	10%
Total Carbohydrate	2g	1%
Dietary Fiber	0.3g	1%
Total Sugars	1.2g	
Protein	37.5g	

131. Sundried Tomato Salmon

 Prep: 15 Minutes | **Cook Time:** 12 Minutes | **Makes:** 1 Serving

INGREDIENTS

- 110g raw salmon
- 25g fresh parsley, chopped
- 1 tablespoon Sun-Dried Tomato Dressing
- Oil for greasing
- Required salt

- Black pepper to taste
- 2 Cherry tomatoes
- 125g broccoli

DIRECTIONS

- Preheat the air fryer to 180°C.
- Prepare a bowl with parsley, dressing, salt, and pepper.
- Spray the fish with oil spray and add the above mixture to the fish.
- Place the salmon fillets with the veggies in the air fryer basket.
- Set it to AIRFRY mode for 12 minutes at 200°C.
- Serve the yummy fish once it is cooked.

 NUTRITION FACTS

Servings: 1

Amount per serving
Calories 215

% Daily Value*
Total Fat	7.8g	10%
Saturated Fat	1.1g	5%
Cholesterol	50mg	17%
Sodium	85mg	4%
Total Carbohydrate	13.6g	5%
Dietary Fiber	4.7g	17%
Total Sugars	7.4g	
Protein	25.9g	

132. Salmon With Dill Dressing

 Prep: 15 Minutes | **Cook Time:** 18 Minutes | **Makes:** 2 Servings

INGREDIENTS

- 2 Salmon fillets
- 2 teaspoons fresh dill
- Salt , to taste
- Black pepper to taste
- For Dill Sauce,
- 60ml low fat plain Greek yogurt
- 2 teaspoons Dijon mustard
- 5ml lemon juice
- 15g chopped fresh dill

DIRECTIONS

- Take a mixing bowl to add all the ingredients for dill sauce and mix it well.
- Place the salmon fillet on a foil sheet.
- Now season the fish with dill, salt, and pepper.
- Seal the Salmon fillet by wrapping the foil.
- Cook the fish for 18 minutes in an air fryer basket at 175°C.

- Air fried Salmon is now ready to eat.
- Serve the fish with Dill sauce and enjoy.

 NUTRITION FACTS

Servings: 2

Amount per serving
Calories 261

% Daily Value*
Total Fat	11.8g	15%
Saturated Fat	2g	10%
Cholesterol	80mg	27%
Sodium	224mg	10%
Total Carbohydrate	2g	1%
Dietary Fiber	0.3g	1%
Total Sugars	1.2g	
Protein	37.5g	

133. Lemon Tilapia Parmesan

 Prep: 12 Minutes | **Cook Time:** 15 Minutes | **Makes:** 2 Servings

INGREDIENTS

- 450g Tilapia or codfish fillet
- 15ml olive oil
- 2 cloves of garlic, chopped
- Salt, to taste
- Black pepper, to taste
- 1 dash of cayenne pepper
- 15ml lemon juice
- 60g shredded parmesan cheese

DIRECTIONS

- Clean the fish fillet and pat dry with a paper towel.
- In a small bowl, mix together the cayenne pepper, lemon juice, chopped garlic, olive oil, salt, and black pepper.
- Brush the mixture over the fish fillet.
- Place the fillet in the air fryer basket and cook for 15 minutes at 180°C.
- Sprinkle the shredded parmesan cheese on top and serve.

 NUTRITION FACTS

Servings: 2

Amount per serving
Calories:	204	
Total Fat:	16.1g	(21% of daily value)
Saturated Fat:	7.1g	(35% of daily value)
Cholesterol:	30mg	(10% of daily value)
Sodium:	570mg	(25% of daily value)

Total Carbohydrate: 12.2g   (4% of daily value)
Dietary Fiber: 0.6g   (2% of daily value)
Protein: 13.8g

134. Lean And Green Salmon

 Prep:
15 Minutes

 Cook Time:
16 Minutes

Makes:
1 Serving

INGREDIENTS

- 450g Salmon fillet
- 60g ricotta cheese
- 1 green onion, chopped
- 2 cloves of garlic, chopped
- 1/4 teaspoon of red pepper
- 2 cherry tomatoes, chopped
- 120g baby spinach
- Salt and black pepper, to taste
- Oil, as needed

DIRECTIONS

- Heat a small amount of oil in a skillet and add the chopped onion, garlic, tomatoes, red pepper, and baby spinach.
- Cook for 2 minutes and add the ricotta cheese.
- Season the salmon fillet with oil, salt, and black pepper.
- Place the salmon fillet on top of the cheese mixture in the skillet.
- Transfer the skillet to the air fryer basket and cook for 16-18 minutes at 200ºC.
- Serve the salmon hot.

NUTRITION FACTS

Servings: 1

Amount per serving

Calories: 779
Total Fat: 34g (44% of daily value)
Saturated Fat: 7.2g (36% of daily value)
Cholesterol: 219mg (73% of daily value)
Sodium: 383mg (17% of daily value)
Total Carbohydrate: 22.3g (8% of daily value)
Dietary Fiber: 6.4g (23% of daily value)
Protein: 101.4g

135. Egg, Shrimp and Avocado

 Prep:
10 Minutes

 Cook Time:
10 Minutes

Makes:
2 Servings

INGREDIENTS

- 1 avocado
- 1 tsp garlic salt
- Oil for greasing
- 1 egg
- 1 tsp paprika powder
- 300g chopped large shrimp

DIRECTIONS

- Preheat the air fryer for 5 minutes at 180ºC.
- Cut the avocado in half, pit it, and scoop out some of the avocado pulp.
- In a mixing bowl, add the eggs, garlic salt, paprika powder, chopped shrimp, and avocado pulp.
- Fill the avocado cavity with the mixture.
- Place the avocados in the air fryer basket.
- Cook for 10 minutes at 200ºC.
- Once cooked, serve and enjoy.

NUTRITION FACTS

Servings: 2

Amount per serving

Calories: 507
Total Fat: 21.8g 28%
Saturated Fat: 4.8g 24%
Cholesterol: 562mg 187%
Sodium: 457mg 20%
Total Carbohydrate: 15g 5%
Dietary Fiber: 6.8g 24%
Total Sugars: 0.7g
Protein: 67.7g

136. Fish Nuggets

 Prep:
12 Minutes

 Cook Time:
8-10 Minutes

 Makes:
2 Servings

INGREDIENTS

- 60ml honey
- 100g croutons
- 1 large egg
- 1/4 tsp chipotle pepper
- Sea salt
- 450g salmon fillet
- Oil for greasing

DIRECTIONS

- Combine honey and chipotle pepper in a saucepan and simmer for 10 minutes.
- Pulse croutons in a mini food processor.
- Whisk the egg in a mixing bowl.
- Preheat the air fryer to 200°C for a few minutes.
- Season the salmon with salt.
- Dip the salmon into the egg mixture and then into the crouton mixture.
- Spray oil in the air fryer basket.
- Cook in the air fryer for 8 minutes.
- Once done, serve the fish nuggets with the sauce.

 NUTRITION FACTS

Servings:	2	
Amount per serving		
Calories	586	
Total Fat	24.3g	31%
Saturated Fat	4g	20%
Cholesterol	193mg	64%
Sodium	241mg	10%
Total Carbohydrate	46.2g	17%
Dietary Fiber	0.9g	3%
Total Sugars	35g	
Protein	49.1g	

08 | **Snacks, Sandwiches And wraps Air Fryer** Recipes

137. Turkey Croquettes

 Prep:
15 Minutes
 Cook Time:
5 Minutes
 Makes:
2 Servings

INGREDIENTS

- 225g mashed potatoes
- 50g grated Parmesan cheese
- 50g shredded Swiss cheese
- 1 finely chopped shallot
- 2 teaspoons (10ml) minced fresh rosemary
- 1 teaspoon (5ml) minced fresh sage
- Salt, to taste
- 1/4 teaspoon (1.25ml) pepper
- 675g finely chopped cooked turkey
- 1 large egg
- 2 tablespoons (30ml) water
- 120g Panko breadcrumbs
- Butter-flavored cooking spray
- Sour cream (optional)

DIRECTIONS

- Preheat the air fryer to to 200°C.
- In a large bowl, add the mashed potatoes, cheeses, shallot, rosemary, sage, salt and pepper.
- Add turkey and make patties.
- In a small bowl, whisk egg and water. Place bread crumbs in another bowl.
- Dip croquettes in egg, and then in bread crumbs mixture.
- Arrange croquettes in the air-fryer basket.
- Cook for 5 minutes, flipping half way through.
- Once it is golden brown, serve with sour cream.

 NUTRITION FACTS

Servings:	2	
Amount per serving		
Calories	1087	
Total Fat	55.8g	72%
Saturated Fat	30.7g	154%
Cholesterol	367mg	122%
Sodium	1256mg	55%
Total Carbohydrate	50.5g	18%
Dietary Fiber	0.7g	3%
Protein	95.6g	

138. Tortellini with Prosciutto

Prep:
15 Minutes
Cook Time:
5-8 Minutes
Makes:
2 Servings

INGREDIENTS

- 1 tablespoon (15ml) olive oil
- 3 tablespoons (45ml) finely chopped onion
- 4 chopped garlic cloves
- 1 can tomato puree
- 1 tablespoon (15ml) minced fresh basil
- 1/4 teaspoon (1.25ml) salt
- 1/4 teaspoon (1.25ml) pepper

Tortellini Ingredients

- 2 large eggs
- 2 tablespoons (30ml) 2% milk
- 165g seasoned bread crumbs
- 1 teaspoon (5ml) garlic powder
- 2 tablespoons (30ml) grated Pecorino Romano cheese
- 1 tablespoon (15ml) minced fresh parsley
- 1/2 teaspoon (2.5ml) salt

- 1 package refrigerated prosciutto ricotta tortellini
- Cooking spray

DIRECTIONS

- Heat oil in a saucepan.
- Add onion and garlic and cook for 3-4 minutes.
- Then add tomato puree, basil, salt and pepper and cook.
- Now preheat the air fryer to to 200ºC.
- Whisk eggs and milk together in a bowl.
- Add bread crumbs, garlic powder, cheese, parsley and salt in a separate bowl.
- Dip tortellini in the egg wash then coats in bread crumb mixture.
- Arrange tortellini in the air-fryer basket.
- Cook for 3-5 minutes. And flip and use cooking spray.
- Once it is completely cooked, serve with sauce and fresh basil.

NUTRITION FACTS

Servings: 2

Amount per serving

Calories	691	
Total Fat	31g	40%
Saturated Fat	13.2g	66%
Cholesterol	247mg	82%
Sodium	1869mg	81%
Total Carbohydrate	72.2g	26%

139. Air-Fryer Beefy Swiss Bundles

 Prep: 15 Minutes **Cook Time:** 12 Minutes **Makes:** 2 Servings

INGREDIENTS

- 450g ground beef
- 225g sliced fresh mushrooms
- 125g chopped onion
- 2 cloves of garlic, chopped
- 4 teaspoons Worcestershire sauce
- 1.8g crushed dried rosemary
- 1.8g paprika
- 2.5g salt
- 0.6g pepper
- 1 sheet frozen puff pastry
- 170g refrigerated mashed potatoes
- 225g shredded Swiss cheese
- 1 large egg
- 30ml water

DIRECTIONS

- Preheat air fryer to 190ºC.
- Cook beef, mushrooms and onion over medium heat for 8-10 minutes in a frying pan.
- Crumble meat and add garlic and cook for a minute.
- Season with Worcestershire sauce, salt, pepper, paprika and rosemary.
- Roll out the pastries and place about 30g of potatoes on each. Top each with 185g of beef mixture and sprinkle with 60g of cheese.
- Brush egg mixture on pastry edges.
- Place the pastries in the air-fryer basket and cook until golden brown for 10-12 minutes.
- Once done, serve and enjoy.

NUTRITION FACTS

Servings: 2

Amount per serving

Calories	1559	

% Daily Value*

Total Fat	31.2g	40%
Saturated Fat	13.8g	69%
Cholesterol	97mg	32%
Sodium	2367mg	103%
Total Carbohydrate	273.9g	100%
Dietary Fiber	12.6g	45%
Total Sugars	39.6g	
Protein	45.6g	

140. Air-Fryer Caribbean Wontons

 Prep: 15 Minutes **Cook Time:** 20 Minutes **Makes:** 2 Servings

INGREDIENTS

- 113g cream cheese
- 60g sweetened shredded coconut
- 60g mashed banana
- 30g chopped walnuts
- 30g canned crushed pineapple
- 225g marshmallow crème
- 24 wonton wrappers
- Cooking spray
- Ingredients for sauce,
- 450g fresh strawberries
- 60g sugar
- 1 tsp cornstarch
- Confectioners' sugar
- Cinnamon

DIRECTIONS

- Preheat air fryer to 150°C. Whip the cream cheese and add coconut, banana, walnuts and pineapple and marshmallow crème in a bowl.
- Place the filling in the wonton wrapper. Fold and seal the wrapper. Repeat with remaining batches.
- Place the wontons in a single layer in the air-fryer basket, spritz with cooking spray.
- Cook until crisp for 11-12 minutes.
- While cooking, add sugar and cornstarch to a saucepan and add the pureed strawberries. Cook until it thickens.
- Use confectioners' sugar and ground cinnamon as toppings.
- Serve wontons with sauce and enjoy.

 NUTRITION FACTS

Servings:	2	
Amount per serving		
Calories	1863	
% Daily Value*		
Total Fat	68.1g	87%
Saturated Fat	50.4g	252%
Cholesterol	35mg	12%
Sodium	22mg	96%
Total Carbohydrate	272.4g	99%
Dietary Fiber	12.6g	45%
Total Sugars	39.5g	
Protein	41.3g	

141. Air-Fryer Bacon Crescent Rolls

 Prep: 12 Minutes **Cook Time:** 6 Minutes **Makes:** 2 Servings

INGREDIENTS

- 250g pizza crust
- 100g thinly sliced ham
- 1 thinly sliced pear
- 60g toasted walnuts
- 30ml crumbled blue cheese

DIRECTIONS

- Preheat the air fryer to 204°C.
- Cut the pizza crust into 4 squares.
- Layer ham, half of the pear slices, walnuts, and blue cheese to form a triangle and press the edges to seal with a fork.

- Arrange the rolls in the air-fryer basket. Cook for 6 minutes.
- Serve with remaining pear slices and enjoy.

 NUTRITION FACTS

Servings:	2	
Amount per serving		
Calories:	399	
Total Fat:	22.7g	(29% Daily Value)
Saturated Fat:	4.4g	(22% Daily Value)
Cholesterol:	69mg	(23% Daily Value)
Sodium:	1028mg	(45% Daily Value)
Total Carbohydrate:	44.5g	(16% Daily Value)
Dietary Fiber:	6g	(21% Daily Value)
Total Sugars:	11g	
Protein:	17.3g	

142. Air Fryer Pumpkin Fries

Prep: 15 Minutes | **Cook Time:** 8 Minutes | **Makes:** 2 Servings

INGREDIENTS

- 125g plain Greek yogurt
- 30ml maple syrup
- 6g chopped chipotle peppers
- Salt to taste
- 1 medium pie pumpkin
- 1g garlic powder
- 1g ground cumin
- 1g chili powder
- 1g pepper

DIRECTIONS

- Preheat the air fryer to 204°C.
- In a small bowl, combine the yogurt, maple syrup, chipotle peppers, and a pinch of salt and refrigerate for a few hours.
- Cut the pumpkin into half slices.
- Sprinkle with salt, garlic powder, cumin, chili powder, and pepper.
- In batches, arrange the pumpkin on a greased tray in the air-fryer basket.
- Cook for 6-8 minutes or until browned.
- Serve with the sauce and enjoy.

NUTRITION FACTS

Servings:	2	
Amount per serving		
Calories:	107	
Total Fat:	0.3g	(0% Daily Value)
Saturated Fat:	0.1g	(0% Daily Value)
Cholesterol:	0mg	(0% Daily Value)

Sodium:	101mg	(4% Daily Value)
Total Carbohydrate:	22.3g	(8% Daily Value)
Dietary Fiber:	1.7g	(6% Daily Value)
Total Sugars:	15.3g	
Protein:	5.7g	

143. Air-Fryer Cheeseburger Onion Rings

 Prep: 25 Minutes   **Cook Time:** 15 Minutes   **Makes:** 2 Servings

INGREDIENTS:

- 450g lean ground beef
- 80ml ketchup
- 30ml mustard
- 2.5ml salt
- 1 large onion
- 115g cheddar cheese
- 175g all-purpose flour
- 2 tspl garlic powder
- 2 large eggs
- 225g panko bread crumbs
- Cooking spray
- Spicy ketchup (optional)

DIRECTIONS:

- Preheat the air fryer to 204°C.
- Cut the onion into 1/2-inch thick slices and separate into rings.
- In a bowl, combine the ground beef, ketchup, mustard, and salt.
- Fill half of the onion rings with the beef mixture and top each with a square of cheese and the remaining beef.
- In a small bowl, mix the flour and garlic powder. Place the eggs and breadcrumbs in separate bowls.
- Dip the filled onion rings in flour to coat both sides, then dip in egg, and finally in breadcrumbs.
- In batches, place the onion rings in the air-fryer basket and spray with cooking spray.
- Cook until golden brown, approximately 12-15 minutes.
- Serve with spicy ketchup and enjoy.

🍲 NUTRITION FACTS (PER SERVING)

Calories:	1238	
Total Fat:	44.9g	(58% of daily value)
Saturated Fat:	19.8g	(99% of daily value)
Cholesterol:	448mg	(149% of daily value)
Sodium:	1999mg	(87% of daily value)
Total Carbohydrates:	98.8g	(36% of daily value)
Dietary Fiber:	7.4g	(26% of daily value)
Total Sugars:	17.9g	
Protein:	106.1g	

144. Air Fryer Toasted Turkey Sandwich Melt

 Prep: 0 Minutes   **Cook Time:** 8 Minutes   **Makes:** 2 Servings

INGREDIENTS:

- 2 ciabatta rolls
- 8 tablespoons mayonnaise
- 6-8 slices peppered turkey
- 4 slices mild cheddar cheese
- 4 slices cooked bacon, cut in half
- 1 thinly sliced Roma tomato
- 1 ripe avocado
- 8-10 pepperoncini peppers
- Spring mix lettuce
- Mustard
- Coarse black pepper to taste

DIRECTIONS:

- Preheat the air fryer to 204°C for 5 minutes.
- Spread 1 tablespoon of mayonnaise on each ciabatta roll.
- Place the sandwich rolls in the air fryer basket and bake for 2 minutes.
- Remove the basket from the air fryer and place cheese on the sandwich rolls.
- Place a few slices of turkey meat on the bottom half of the rolls and top with 2 slices of precooked bacon.
- Place the basket back in the air fryer and cook until the cheese is melted, approximately 2-3 minutes.
- Remove the sandwich and layer with avocado, pepperoncini, tomatoes, spring mix lettuce, and condiments.
- Cut the sandwiches and serve.

145. Air Fryer Veggie Sandwich

 Prep: 10 Minutes   **Cook Time:** 8 Minutes   **Serves:** 2

INGREDIENTS

- 100g grated cheese
- A few mushroom slices
- A few slices of red bell pepper
- A large spoonful of pesto
- 1 cherry tomato, quartered

- 2 slices of bread
- A little olive oil

INSTRUCTIONS

- Brush oil on the mushrooms and peppers, then air fry for 5 minutes at 200ºC.
- Assemble the sandwich by spreading pesto on the bread and filling with cheese, mushrooms, pepper, and tomato.
- Brush olive oil on the outer sides of the bread and sprinkle a little extra cheese on top.
- Air fry for 5 minutes at 200ºC until the bread is crispy.
- Serve the veggie toast.

NUTRITION INFORMATION

Servings:	2	
Per serving:		
Calories	150	
Total Fat	12g	15%
Saturated Fat	2.9g	14%
Cholesterol	7mg	2%
Sodium	107mg	5%
Total Carbohydrate	7.9g	3%
Dietary Fiber	1.2g	4%
Total Sugars	2.2g	
Protein	3.5g	

146. Air Fryer Aubergine Parmesan Sandwich

 Prep: 20 Minutes | **Cook Time:** 15 Minutes | **Serves:** 2

INGREDIENTS

- 50g Italian bread crumbs
- 25g Panko bread crumbs
- 25g grated Parmesan cheese
- 1 tsp Italian seasoning
- 1 tsp salt
- ½ tsp garlic powder
- ½ tsp freshly ground black pepper
- 25g plain flour
- 2 eggs
- 1 sliced aubergine
- Olive oil spray
- 100g spaghetti sauce
- 8 slices mozzarella cheese
- Buns/Sliders
- Fresh basil, optional

INSTRUCTIONS

- Mix both types of bread crumbs, Italian seasoning, cheese, garlic powder, and black pepper.
- Keep the flour on a separate plate and the beaten eggs in a shallow dish.
- Coat the sliced aubergine in the flour, beaten eggs, and breadcrumb mixture.
- Spray oil on the coated aubergine.
- Preheat the air fryer to 200ºC.
- Place the breaded aubergine rounds in the air fryer basket and cook for 8 minutes, flipping each round, until crispy.
- Top each cooked aubergine slice with spaghetti sauce and 1 slice of mozzarella cheese.
- Place the basket back in the air fryer and cook until the cheese starts to melt, 2 more minutes.
- Repeat the same process for the remaining aubergine.
- Assemble the sandwich by placing 2 aubergine parmesan slices in each toasted bun.
- Top with fresh basil and extra warmed sauce as desired.

147. Crispy Chicken Caesar Wraps

 Prep: 10 Minutes | **Cook Time:** 8 Minutes | **Makes:** 2 Servings

INGREDIENTS

- 8 ounces chicken breast
- 2 eggs
- 125g plain flour
- 30g cornflour
- 3 tbsp mixed herbs
- 60ml light Caesar dressing
- 30g grated parmesan cheese
- 50g croutons
- 1 head of romaine lettuce
- 4 - 20cm tortilla wraps

DIRECTIONS

- Mix the plain flour, cornflour and mixed herbs together in a bowl.
- Beat the eggs in a separate bowl.
- Dip the chicken strips in the flour mixture, then the beaten eggs and then back into the flour mixture, ensuring they are well coated.

- Spray cooking oil in the air fryer basket and place the battered chicken strips in it.
- Cook at 204°C for 8 minutes, flip and cook for a further 3 minutes.
- Mix the lettuce, dressing, cheese and croutons together in a bowl.
- Place 1/2 cup of the salad mixture and 3-4 chicken strips in each tortilla wrap.
- Roll up the wrap, like a burrito, and serve.

 NUTRITION FACTS

Servings:	2	
Amount per serving		
Calories	697	
% Daily Value*		
Total Fat	15.5g	20%
Saturated Fat	5.7g	28%
Cholesterol	256mg	85%
Sodium	413mg	18%
Total Carbohydrate	89.9g	33%
Dietary Fiber	5.9g	21%
Total Sugars	2.6g	
Protein	48.6g	

148. Air Fried Pepperoni Wraps

 Prep: 10 Minutes | **Cook Time:** 5 Minutes | **Makes:** 2 Servings

INGREDIENTS

- 2 flour tortilla wraps
- 28 pepperoni slices
- 2 slices cooked and crumbled bacon
- 30g mozzarella cheese
- 30g mature cheddar cheese

DIRECTIONS

- Place 14 pepperoni slices on each of the tortilla wraps.
- Sprinkle 1 piece of crumbled bacon and 15g of mozzarella cheese on each wrap.
- Then sprinkle 15g of mature cheddar cheese on each wrap.
- Wrap up the tortilla and place, seam side down, in the air fryer basket.
- Spray with cooking oil.
- Cook in the air fryer at 204°C for 3-5 minutes until the cheese is melted.
- Serve and enjoy.

 NUTRITION FACTS

Servings:	2	
Amount per serving		
Calories	1228	
% Daily Value*		
Total Fat	94.9g	122%
Saturated Fat	33.5g	167%
Cholesterol	243mg	81%
Sodium	4431mg	193%
Total Carbohydrate	13.6g	5%
Dietary Fiber	1.5g	5%
Total Sugars	0.3g	
Protein	75.6g	

149. 5-Minute Buffalo Chicken Wrap

 Prep: 15 Minutes | **Cook Time:** 5 Minutes | **Makes:** 2 Servings

INGREDIENTS

- 300g Leftover Chicken
- 120ml Buffalo Sauce
- 4 Flour Tortillas
- 60g Chunky Blue Cheese
- 60g Shredded Lettuce
- Shredded Cheddar Cheese

DIRECTIONS

- Chop up chicken into smaller pieces and add to a bowl.
- Pour the buffalo sauce over the chicken and mix thoroughly.
- Place the chicken in the air fryer and cook for 5 minutes at 200°C.
- Fill each tortilla with buffalo chicken, blue cheese, and lettuce.
- Wrap each tortilla and serve with shredded cheddar cheese as an additional topping.

 NUTRITION FACTS

Servings:	2	
Amount per serving		
Calories:	897	
Total Fat:	63.2g	(81%)
Saturated Fat:	14.9g	(75%)
Cholesterol:	264mg	(88%)
Sodium:	1322mg	(57%)
Total Carbohydrates:	4.7g	(2%)
Dietary Fiber:	0g	
Total Sugars:	4.2g	
Protein:	73.4g	

150. Beef and Cheese Wrap

 Prep: 15 Minutes   **Cook Time:** 20 Minutes   **Makes:** 2 Servings

INGREDIENTS

- 450g Ground Beef
- 225g Shredded Cabbage
- 85g Cheddar Cheese
- 6 Flour Tortillas
- 3-4 Garlic Cloves
- Zest and Juice of 1 Lime
- 1 Sweet Bell Pepper
- 60ml Sour Cream
- 15ml Taco Seasoning

DIRECTIONS

- Chop the garlic and cube the sweet bell pepper.
- In a bowl, mix the shredded cabbage, half the sour cream, and half the taco seasoning.
- In another bowl, mix the diced pepper, garlic, lime zest, and juice.
- Place the beef and taco seasoning in the basket of the air fryer, sprayed with oil.
- Cook for 18 minutes at 200ºC.
- Fill each tortilla with diced pepper, cabbage slaw, ground beef, and cheddar cheese.
- Serve and enjoy the beef wrap.

NUTRITION FACTS

Servings: 2

Amount per serving

Calories:	1271	
Total Fat:	46.3g	(59%)
Saturated Fat:	20.1g	(100%)
Cholesterol:	489mg	(163%)
Sodium:	509mg	(22%)
Total Carbohydrates:	40.1g	(15%)
Dietary Fiber:	6.2g	(22%)
Total Sugars:	4.9g	
Protein:	165.7g	

151. Air-Fried Cheesy Spinach Wrap

 Prep: 15 Minutes   **Cook Time:** 15 Minutes   **Makes:** 2 Servings

INGREDIENTS

- 180g cooked roughly chopped spinach
- 1 wedge creamy Swiss cheese
- 1/4 tsp garlic powder
- 3 - 4 chopped sun-dried tomato halves
- 2 flour tortilla
- 1 stick light string cheese

DIRECTIONS

- Add the cooked spinach, cheese wedge, and garlic powder to a microwave-safe bowl and cook for 1 minute.
- Combine until cheese has melted and mixture is uniform. And now add chopped sun-dried tomatoes.
- Spread mixture along the center of the tortilla. Add cheese over the spinach mixture.
- Wrap the tortilla like a burrito then keep the wrap inside the air fryer by facing the seam side down.
- Cook for 5 minutes at 200ºC.
- Serve and enjoy.

NUTRITION FACTS

Servings: 2

Amount per serving
Calories   131

% Daily Value*

Total Fat	6.5g	8%
Saturated Fat	3.6g	18%
Cholesterol	19mg	6%
Sodium	140mg	6%
Total Carbohydrate	12g	4%
Dietary Fiber	1.5g	6%
Total Sugars	0.4g	
Protein	7.6g	

152. Air-Fried Chicken Shawarma

 Prep: 25 Minutes   **Cook Time:** 15 Minutes   **Makes:** 4 Servings

INGREDIENTS

- 900g chicken thighs
- 30ml olive oil
- 1 lemon, juiced and zested
- 8 crushed cloves garlic
- 30ml honey
- 10g ground cumin
- 10g smoked paprika
- 5g ground cinnamon
- 5g coriander powder
- 5g ground ginger
- 5g dried oregano
- 5g ground turmeric
- 2.5g cayenne pepper
- 10g salt
- 5g ground black pepper
- 4 shawarma wraps

DIRECTIONS

- Clean the chicken and pat dry.
- Put the chicken thighs in a bowl and add all the above ingredients and mix it well.
- Keep the marinated chicken in the fridge for at least 30 minutes.
- Place the chicken in the air fryer basket for 10-15 minutes at 200°C.
- Repeat the same process for the remaining chicken thighs.
- Serve and enjoy.

 NUTRITION FACTS

Servings:	4	
Amount per serving		
Calories	538	
% Daily Value*		
Total Fat	24.3g	62%
Saturated Fat	5.7g	57%
Cholesterol	202mg	135%
Sodium	198.5mg	17%
Total Carbohydrate	11.5g	4%
Dietary Fiber	1.35g	10%
Total Sugars	8.8g	

09 Pizzas & Bread

153. Air Fried Cauliflower Pizza Crust

 Prep: 20 Minutes | **Cook Time:** 20 Minutes | **Makes:** 2 Servings

INGREDIENTS

- For crust,
- 450g head of cauliflower
- 115g of shredded mozzarella
- 55g grated Parmesan
- 1 tsp dried oregano
- 1 tsp kosher salt
- 1/4 tsp garlic powder
- 2 eggs, lightly beaten
- For toppings
- 60g Pizza sauce
- A few Pepperoni
- A few Mushrooms
- 75g Mozzarella

DIRECTIONS

- Finely cut the cauliflower florets and pulse them in the food processor.
- Then cook the cauliflower in a steamer. And drain the cauliflower.
- Add the mozzarella, Parmesan, oregano, salt, garlic powder, and eggs to the mixing bowl.
- Now add the cauliflower to the mixture and switch to the parchment paper and make a pizza shape.
- Keep the pizza in the air fryer and set the timer to 350 degrees Fahrenheit or 170 degrees C, for 14 minutes.
- Once the pizza crust is baked, add the pizza sauce on both sides of the pizza crust.
- Add mozzarella cheese to the crust and then add pepperoni and mushrooms.
- Now keep the pizza back in the air fryer and set the time for 4 minutes at 350 degrees Fahrenheit or 170 degrees C.

NUTRITION FACTS

Servings:	2	
Amount per serving		
Calories	201	
% Daily Value*		
Total Fat	11.6g	15%
Saturated Fat	4.6g	23%
Cholesterol	182mg	61%
Sodium	949mg	41%
Total Carbohydrate	11.3g	4%
Dietary Fiber	4g	14%
Total Sugars	4.5g	
Protein	15.1g	

154. Vegan Pizza Crust Mix

 Prep: 15 Minutes | **Cook Time:** 25 Minutes | **Makes:** 2 Servings

INGREDIENTS

- 225g quinoa or millet
- 1 tsp dried oregano
- 1 tsp dried basil
- 1 tsp garlic powder
- 1/2 tsp dried rosemary
- Required salt
- Toppings
- 120g Marinara sauce
- A few slices of Vegan cheese
- 6 Kalamata olives
- 2 artichoke hearts
- 1 small thinly sliced onion
- A few banana peppers
- Spinach, a few leaves
- Basil micro greens

DIRECTIONS

- For the crust:
- Soak the quinoa with water overnight.
- Strain off the water and pulse the drained quinoa/millet in a blender with water and the remaining ingredients, excluding toppings.
- For the pizza,
- Apply oil in the baking pan.
- Put the pizza crust batter in the pan and set the air fryer at 350 degrees F or 170 degrees C, for 18-20 minutes.
- Once it's half cooked, gently flip the crust over. And bake for another 13-15 minutes at 350 degrees.
- Take the pizza out of the air fryer and top it with the toppings.
- Then air fry for 5-6 minutes at 400 degrees or 204 degrees C.
- Enjoy the pizza with basil microgreens and enjoy!

 NUTRITION FACTS

Servings: 2

Amount per serving
Calories 934

% Daily Value*

Total Fat	53.7g	69%
Saturated Fat	23.8g	119%
Cholesterol	1mg	0%
Sodium	1142mg	50%
Total Carbohydrate	91.5g	33%
Dietary Fiber	18.4g	66%
Total Sugars	9g	
Protein	24	

155. Grilled Chicken Pizza

 Prep: 25 Minutes | **Cook Time:** 19-20 Minutes | **Makes:** 2 Servings

INGREDIENTS

- 225g of grilled chicken breasts
- 15ml olive oil
- 25cm pizza dough
- 80ml prepared pesto
- 1 large tomato, chopped
- 100g shredded mozzarella cheese

DIRECTIONS

- roll the dough on a flat area and grease it with oil spray.
- Keep it on the baking pan.

- Turn to pizza mode and set the air fryer to 170°C, for 10 minutes.
- Flip the pizza when it's half-baked.
- And take out the pizza and put pesto.
- Then top with grilled chicken, tomatoes, and mozzarella cheese.
- Then continue baking the pizza, by placing it inside the air fryer.
- Switch to pizza mode and set the air fryer to 204°C, for 9 minutes.
- When the cheese starts melting, serve the pizza and enjoy.

 NUTRITION FACTS

Servings: 2

Amount per serving

Calories	608	
Total Fat	39.6g	51% of the daily value
Saturated Fat	9.2g	46% of the daily value
Cholesterol	36mg	12% of the daily value
Sodium	540mg	23% of the daily value
Total Carbohydrate	44.8g	16% of the daily value
Dietary Fiber	4.4g	16% of the daily value
Total Sugars	2.5g	
Protein	18.9g	

156. Seafood Pizza

 Prep: 20 Minutes | **Cook Time:** 20 Minutes | **Makes:** 2 Servings

INGREDIENTS

- 225g pizza crust
- Oil spray

Topping Ingredients

- 6 uncooked shrimp
- 6 tablespoons of pizza sauce
- 115g shredded mozzarella cheese
- 115g shredded provolone cheese
- 80g of scallops
- 125g chopped fresh basil leaves
- Few chopped garlic cloves

DIRECTIONS

- roll the dough on a flat area and grease it with oil spray.
- Keep it on the baking pan.
- Turn to pizza mode and set the air fryer to 170°C, for 10 minutes.

- Flip the pizza when it's half-baked. And take out the pizza; put pizza sauce over it.
- Then adding toppings with; scallops, shrimp, mozzarella cheese, provolone cheese, garlic, and basil.
- Put the pan in the air fryer and switch to pizza mode at 204°C, for 9 minutes.
- When the cheese starts melting, serve the pizza and enjoy.

 NUTRITION FACTS

Servings: 2

Amount per serving

Calories	668	
Total Fat	24.1g	31% of the daily value
Saturated Fat	13g	65% of the daily value
Cholesterol	193mg	64% of the daily value
Sodium	1791mg	78% of the daily value
Total Carbohydrate	63.3g	23% of the daily value
Dietary Fiber	2.6g	9% of the daily value
Total Sugars	8.7g	
Protein	50g	

157. Grilled Meat Lover Pizza

 Prep: 20 Minutes | **Cook Time:** 18 Minutes | **Makes:** 3 Servings

INGREDIENTS

- 225g of pizza dough
- 2 tablespoons of olive oil
- Toppings
- 80ml pizza sauce
- 355g shredded mozzarella cheese
- 225g cooked and crumbled sausage
- 10 pepperoni slices
- 6 slices of bacon, cooked and sliced
- 60g shredded Parmesan cheese

DIRECTIONS

- Roll the dough on a flat area and grease it with oil spray.
- Transfer it to the baking pan or basket.
- Turn to pizza mode and set the air fryer to 170°C, for 10 minutes.
- Flip the pizza when it's half-baked. Take it out of the air fryer, spread the pizza sauce over it.
- Then add the pizza toppings. Place the baking pan back in the air fryer.
- And switch to pizza mode at 204°C for 8 minutes.
- When the cheese starts melting, serve the pizza and enjoy.

 NUTRITION FACTS

Servings: 3

Amount per serving

Calories 941

% Daily Value*

Total Fat	75.6g	95%
Saturated Fat	23.0g	115%
Cholesterol	208mg	69%
Sodium	4467mg	191%
Total Carbohydrate	47.4g	17%
Dietary Fiber	3.7g	13%
Total Sugars	0.3g	
Protein	55.0g	

158. Three Cheese Pizza

 Prep: 20 Minutes | **Cook Time:** 18 Minutes | **Makes:** 2-3 Servings

INGREDIENTS

- 375g of store-bought pizza dough
- 2 tablespoons of olive oil

TOPPING INGREDIENTS

- 240ml marinara sauce
- 180g shredded mozzarella cheese
- 90g shredded Parmesan cheese
- 120g ricotta cheese
- A few basil leaves
- DIRECTIONS
- Roll the dough on a flat area and grease it with oil spray.
- Transfer it to the baking tin or basket of the air fryer, and set the air fryer to 170°C, for 10 minutes.
- Flip the pizza when it's half-baked. Take it out of the air fryer and spread the marinara sauce over it.
- Then add the cheese as toppings. Sprinkle a few basil leaves on top.
- Place the pizza in the air fryer and switch to pizza mode at 204°C, for 8 minutes.
- When the cheese starts melting, serve the pizza and enjoy.

 NUTRITION FACTS

Servings: 2

Amount per serving

Calories 888

% Daily Value*

Total Fat	60.2g	76%
Saturated Fat	17.2g	86%
Cholesterol	41mg	14%
Sodium	3150mg	136%
Total Carbohydrate	72.0g	26%
Dietary Fiber	8.3g	30%
Total Sugars	4.8g	
Protein	26.5g	

159. Sausage Pizza

 Prep: 12 Minutes | **Cook Time:** 18-22 Minutes | **Makes:** 2 Servings

INGREDIENTS

- 284g pizza dough
- 120ml marinara sauce
- 340g cooked and crumbled spicy sausage
- 57g thinly sliced onion
- 450g shredded mozzarella cheese
- 15ml chili oil
- Black pepper, to taste

DIRECTIONS

- Spray olive oil and roll the dough on the baking pan or air fryer basket.
- Turn to pizza mode and set the air fryer to 170°C, for 10 minutes.
- Flip the pizza when it's half-baked. And take out the pizza and spread the marinara sauce over it.
- Now add toppings to the pizza with the sausage, onion, and mozzarella cheese.
- Spray chili oil and sprinkle with pepper.
- Put the pizza in the air fryer and switch to pizza mode at 204°C, for 8 minutes.
- When the cheese starts melting, serve the pizza and enjoy.

NUTRITION FACTS

Servings: 2

Amount per serving

Calories 1575

% Daily Value*

Total Fat	114.3g	147%
Saturated Fat	33g	165%
Cholesterol	159mg	53%
Sodium	2521mg	110%
Total Carbohydrate	82.9g	30%
Dietary Fiber	7.7g	28%
Total Sugars	6.4g	
Protein	52g	

160. Italian Sausage Pizza

 Prep: 20 Minutes | **Cook Time:** 25 Minutes | **Makes:** 2 Servings

INGREDIENTS

- 284g thin-crust pizza dough

Topping Ingredients

- 4 hot cubed Italian sausages
- 57g sliced onion
- 57g chopped mushrooms
- 120ml pizza sauce
- 450g parmesan cheese
- 30ml chili oil
- Black pepper, to taste

DIRECTIONS

- Spray olive oil and roll the dough on the pan or air fryer basket.
- set the air fryer to 170°C, for 10 minutes.
- Now spread pizza sauce, Italian sausage, raw onion, mushrooms, and parmesan cheeses over the pizza.
- Spray chili oil and sprinkle pepper on the pizza.
- Put the pizza in the air fryer and switch to pizza mode at 204°C, for 15 minutes.
- When the cheese starts melting, serve the pizza and enjoy.

NUTRITION FACTS

Servings: 2

Amount per serving

Calories 1728

% Daily Value*

Total Fat	95.7g	123%
Saturated Fat	38.4g	192%
Cholesterol	250mg	83%
Sodium	3597mg	156%
Total Carbohydrate	141.4g	51%
Dietary Fiber	1.8g	6%
Total Sugars	3.5g	
Protein	81.5g	

161. Easy Mix Vegetable Pizza

Prep: 15 Minutes | **Cook Time:** 17-20 Minutes | **Makes:** 2 Servings

INGREDIENTS:

- 450g store-bought pizza dough
- Toppings:
- 225g cream cheese
- 125g mayonnaise
- 1/2 tsp dry ranch dressing
- 225g broccoli
- 4 baby tomatoes
- 60g shredded carrots
- 225g red bell peppers

DIRECTIONS:

- Spray olive oil and roll the dough on the baking pan or basket of an air fryer.
- Turn to pizza mode and set the air fryer to 204°C, for 8 minutes.
- Flip the pizza when it's half-baked.
- Combine mayonnaise, cream cheese, and ranch dressing in a bowl.
- Take the pizza out and spread the ranch mixture along with the remaining toppings.
- Switch to pizza mode and set the air fryer to 204°C, for 9 minutes.
- When the cheese starts melting, serve the pizza and enjoy.
- Nutrition Facts:

Servings: 2

Amount per serving:
Calories: 1054
Total Fat: 88.5g (113% of daily value)
Saturated Fat: 41.3g (207% of daily value)
Cholesterol: 216mg (72% of daily value)
Sodium: 1771mg (77% of daily value)
Total Carbohydrate: 34.6g (13% of daily value)
Dietary Fiber: 2.4g (8% of daily value)
Total Sugars: 8.6g
Protein: 34.8g

162. Ultimate Veggie Pizza

 Prep: 18 Minutes | **Cook Time:** 22 Minutes | **Makes:** 2 Servings

INGREDIENTS:

- 1 batch of store-bought pizza dough

Topping Ingredients:

- 225g pizza sauce or marinara sauce
- 450g baby spinach
- 450g shredded mozzarella cheese
- 120g fresh red bell pepper
- 120g red onion
- 225g halved cherry tomatoes
- 120g pitted Kalamata olives
- 120g sliced almonds
- A few basil leaves
- Italian seasoning

DIRECTIONS:

- Spray olive oil and roll the dough on the baking pan or basket of the air fryer.
- Turn to pizza mode and set the air fryer to 170°C, for 10 minutes.
- Flip the pizza when it's half-baked. Take out the pizza and spread the pizza sauce all over.
- Then add pizza toppings with the listed ingredients.
- Put the pizza in the air fryer and switch to pizza mode at 204°C, for 12 minutes.
- When the cheese starts melting, serve the pizza and enjoy.
- Nutrition Facts:

Servings: 2

Amount per serving:
Calories: 1189
Total Fat: 51.4g (66% of daily value)
Saturated Fat: 12g (60% of daily value)
Cholesterol: 100mg (33% of daily value)
Sodium: 2349mg (102% of daily value)
Total Carbohydrate: 153.3g (56% of daily value)
Dietary Fiber: 7.7g (28% of daily value)
Total Sugars: 7.9g
Protein: 31.9g

163. Veggies Pizza

 Prep: 20 Minutes | **Cook Time:** 15 Minutes | **Makes:** 2 Servings

INGREDIENTS

- 450g store-bought thin-crust pizza dough
- Toppings:
- Salt, to taste
- 225g Japanese eggplant
- 225g thinly sliced yellow squash
- 225g thinly sliced red onion
- 225g thinly sliced yellow bell pepper
- 180g pizza sauce
- 225g shredded mozzarella cheese

DIRECTIONS

- Spray olive oil and roll the dough onto the baking pan.
- Turn to pizza mode and set the air fryer to 204 degrees C for 8 minutes.
- Cook for 8 minutes at 204 degrees C.
- Flip the pizza when it's half-baked. Take out the pizza and spread pizza sauce all over.
- Then add the listed toppings.
- Put the pizza back in the air fryer and cook for 6 minutes at 170 degrees C.
- Take the pizza out and sprinkle cheese on top, and cook for a further 5 minutes.
- When the cheese starts melting, serve the pizza and enjoy.

NUTRITION FACTS

Servings: 2

Amount per serving
Calories 1327

% Daily Value*

Total Fat	51.3g	66%
Saturated Fat	19.6g	98%
Cholesterol	145mg	48%
Sodium	2440mg	106%
Total Carbohydrate	167.5g	61%
Dietary Fiber	13.8g	49%
Total Sugars	17.6g	
Protein	53.2g	

164. Artichoke Pizza

 Prep:
20 Minutes
 Cook Time:
18 Minutes
 Makes:
3 Servings

INGREDIENTS

- 700g store-bought pizza dough
- Oil spray
- Toppings:
- 225g marinara sauce
- 450g thawed baby spinach
- 450g mozzarella cheese
- 225g canned artichoke, drained
- 125g thinly sliced bell pepper
- 125g thin wedged red onion
- 125g cherry tomatoes, halved
- 5g red pepper flakes
- 225g Parmesan cheese

DIRECTIONS

- Spray olive oil and roll the dough on the baking pan. Add it to the air fryer and set the air fryer to 204 degrees C, for 10 minutes.
- Flip the pizza when it's half-baked. Take out the pizza and add the toppings with the above-listed ingredients.
- Now sprinkle with red pepper flakes.
- Place the pizza back in the air fryer and switch to pizza mode at 204 degrees C, for 8 minutes.
- When the cheese starts melting, serve the pizza and enjoy.

NUTRITION FACTS

Servings: 3

Amount per serving
Calories 1261

% Daily Value*

Total Fat	48g	62%
Saturated Fat	18g	90%
Cholesterol	141mg	47%
Sodium	2381mg	104%
Total Carbohydrate	166.4g	60%
Dietary Fiber	15g	54%
Total Sugars	3.7g	
Protein	48.5g	

165. Supreme Pizza

 Prep:
17 Minutes
 Cook Time:
20 Minutes
 Makes:
2 Servings

INGREDIENTS

- 1 pizza dough, store-bought
- 30 ml olive oil
- Topping ingredients
- 6 cremini mushrooms
- 6 slices of white onion
- 3 tablespoons pesto
- 200 g shredded mozzarella
- 1 green pepper
- 100 g spinach
- 12 slices of tomato

DIRECTIONS

- roll the dough on a flat area and grease it with oil spray.
- add to baking tin or basket of air fryer
- set the air fryer to 204 degrees C, for 15 minutes.
- Flip the pizza when it's half-baked. And take out the pizza; and add toppings with mushrooms, pesto, white onion, green pepper, spinach, tomato, and cheese.

- Put the pizza in the air fryer and switch to pizza mode.
- Now cook at 204 degrees C, for 5 minutes.
- When the cheese starts melting, serve the pizza and enjoy.

 NUTRITION FACTS

Servings: 2

Amount per serving

Calories 815

% Daily Value*

Total Fat	59.1g	76%
Saturated Fat	14.4g	72%
Cholesterol	21mg	7%
Sodium	803mg	35%
Total Carbohydrate	55.3g	20%
Dietary Fiber	7g	25%
Total Sugars	7.7g	
Protein	19.3g	

166. Chorizo Pizza

 Prep: 20 Minutes | **Cook Time:** 10 Minutes | **Makes:** 3-4 Servings

INGREDIENTS

- 30 ml of olive oil
- 375 g of thin-crust pizza dough

Topping Ingredients

- 4 tablespoons basil pesto
- 125 ml pizza sauce
- 12 slices chorizo
- ½ sliced yellow pepper
- 2 sliced small red onion
- 12 slices of fresh mozzarella

DIRECTIONS

- roll the dough on a flat area and grease it with oil spray.
- add to baking tin or basket of an air fryer.
- set the air fryer to 204 degrees C , for 5 minutes.
- Flip the pizza when it's half-baked. And take out the pizza; and spread basil pesto, pizza sauce, chorizo, yellow pepper, red onion, and fresh mozzarella.
- Put the pizza back in the air fryer and switch to pizza mode.
- And cook at 204 degrees C, for 5 minutes.

- When the cheese starts melting, serve the pizza and enjoy.

 NUTRITION FACTS

Servings: 3

Amount per serving

Calories 2267

% Daily Value*

Total Fat	147.5g	189%
Saturated Fat	54.3g	272%
Cholesterol	345mg	115%
Sodium	5013mg	218%
Total Carbohydrate	128g	47%
Dietary Fiber	2g	7%
Total Sugars	3.3g	
Protein	104.5g	

167. Simple Air Fryer Pizza

 Prep: 14 minutes | **Cook Time:** 20 minutes | **Serves:** 2

INGREDIENTS

- 250g thin-crust pizza dough
- Oil spray
- Topping ingredients
- 1 small chopped onion
- 125g sliced red sweet pepper
- 125g sliced yellow sweet pepper
- 3 chorizo links
- 80g tomato sauce
- 120g shredded jack cheese

DIRECTIONS

- Roll out the pizza dough on a flat surface and lightly spray with oil.
- Place the dough in the baking tin or basket of the air fryer.
- Set the air fryer to 204°C and cook the dough for 15 minutes.
- Flip the pizza when half-cooked and spread the toppings evenly over the dough, including the chopped onion, sliced red and yellow sweet pepper, chorizo, tomato sauce, and shredded jack cheese.
- Return the pizza to the air fryer and switch to pizza mode.
- Cook the pizza at 204°C for a further 5 minutes.
- Serve the pizza once the cheese has melted and enjoy.

NUTRITION INFORMATION (PER SERVING)

Calories:	996	
Fat:	40.4g	(52%)
Saturated Fat:	19.5g	(98%)
Cholesterol:	90mg	(30%)
Sodium:	1827mg	(79%)
Carbohydrates:	127g	(46%)
Fiber:	11.2g	(40%)
Sugar:	3g	
Protein:	43.7g	

168.White Pizza

 Prep:
20 minutes

 Cook Time:
16 minutes

 Serves:
2

INGREDIENTS

- 250g thin-crust pizza dough
- 1 tablespoon extra virgin olive oil
- Topping ingredients
- 60g ricotta cheese
- 7 slices of fresh mozzarella
- 2 cloves of garlic, minced
- 1 teaspoon red pepper flakes

DIRECTIONS

- Roll out the pizza dough on a flat surface and brush with the extra virgin olive oil.
- Place the dough in the baking tin or basket of the air fryer.
- Set the air fryer to 204°C and cook the dough for 10 minutes.
- Flip the pizza when half-cooked and spread the ricotta cheese evenly over the dough.
- Add the slices of fresh mozzarella, minced garlic, and red pepper flakes as toppings.
- Return the pizza to the air fryer and switch to pizza mode.
- Cook the pizza at 204°C for a further 6 minutes.
- Serve the pizza once the cheese has melted and enjoy.

 NUTRITION INFORMATION (PER SERVING)

Calories:	1230	
Fat:	33.1g	(42%)
Saturated Fat:	13.1g	(65%)
Cholesterol:	62mg	(21%)
Sodium:	1535mg	(67%)
Carbohydrates:	168.6g	(61%)
Fiber:	6.3g	(23%)
Sugar:	0.2g	
Protein:	61.8g	

169.Air Fryer Pizza

 Prep:
15 Minutes

 Cook Time:
20 Minutes

 Serves:
2

INGREDIENTS:

- 450g fresh homemade pizza dough

Topping Ingredients:
- 60ml pizza sauce
- 12 slices pepperoni, as needed
- 120g mozzarella cheese
- 1 tsp Italian seasoning

INSTRUCTIONS:

- Roll out the dough on a flat surface and lightly spray with oil.
- Place the dough in the basket of the air fryer and set the temperature to 204°C. Bake for 10 minutes.
- Flip the pizza dough and add the pizza sauce, spreading it evenly over the surface.
- Sprinkle the Italian seasoning, pepperoni and mozzarella cheese over the pizza.
- Return the pizza to the air fryer and set the temperature to 204°C. Bake for 10 minutes.
- When the cheese is melted and bubbly, remove the pizza from the air fryer and serve hot.

 NUTRITION INFORMATION (PER SERVING):

Calories:	726	
Total Fat:	19.4g	(25% of daily value)
Saturated Fat:	3.4g	(17%)
Cholesterol:	23mg	(8%)
Sodium:	1631mg	(71%)
Total Carbohydrates:	124g	(45%)
Dietary Fiber:	10.5g	(38%)
Total Sugars:	1.2g	
Protein:	26.3g	

170.Salami Pizza

 Prep:
20 Minutes

 Cook Time:
20 Minutes

 Serves:
2

INGREDIENTS:

- 450g pizza dough
- 30ml vegetable oil

Topping Ingredients:

- 120g mozzarella cheese
- 50g salami strips
- 6 sliced mushrooms
- 1 tsp dried oregano
- freshly ground black pepper, to taste
- 4 tbsp grated Parmesan cheese
- a handful of fresh arugula

INSTRUCTIONS:

- Roll out the pizza dough on a flat surface and lightly spray with oil.
- Place the dough in the basket of the air fryer and set the temperature to 204°C. Bake for 10 minutes.
- Flip the pizza dough and add the toppings: mozzarella cheese, salami strips, sliced mushrooms, dried oregano, black pepper, grated Parmesan cheese, and arugula.
- Return the pizza to the air fryer and set the temperature to 204°C. Bake for 10 minutes.
- When the cheese is melted and bubbly, remove the pizza from the air fryer and serve hot.

NUTRITION INFORMATION (PER SERVING):

Calories:	764	
Total Fat:	56.5g	(72% of daily value)
Saturated Fat:	17.4g	(87%)
Cholesterol:	42mg	(14%)
Sodium:	1058mg	(46%)
Total Carbohydrates:	45g	(16%)
Dietary Fiber:	4.2g	(15%)
Total Sugars:	1.5g	
Protein:	21.5g	

171. Pepperoni Pizza

 Prep Time: 20 Minutes   **Cook Time:** 16 Minutes   **Serves:** 2

INGREDIENTS:

- 450g store-bought pizza dough
- Oil spray for greasing
- Toppings:
- 80ml marinara sauce
- 25g shredded mozzarella cheese
- 25g shredded cheddar cheese
- 10 slices of pepperoni
- 1 tsp chopped parsley

INSTRUCTIONS:

- Roll the dough on a flat surface and lightly grease it with the oil spray.
- Place the dough in the baking tin or basket of the air fryer and set the temperature to 400 degrees Fahrenheit (204 degrees Celsius) for 10 minutes.
- Once half-baked, remove the pizza and spread the marinara sauce evenly over it.
- Add the mozzarella cheese, cheddar cheese, pepperoni slices, and parsley as toppings.
- Place the pizza back in the air fryer and set the temperature to 400 degrees Fahrenheit (204 degrees Celsius) for 6 minutes.
- Serve once the cheese has melted.

NUTRITION INFORMATION:

Servings:	2	
Per serving:		
Calories:	276	
Fat:	18.2g	(23% of daily value)
Saturated Fat:	7.5g	(37% of daily value)
Cholesterol:	46mg	(15% of daily value)
Sodium:	639mg	(28% of daily value)
Carbohydrates:	13.9g	(5% of daily value)
Fiber:	0.5g	(2% of daily value)
Sugars:	0.1g	
Protein:	13.3g	

172. Garlic Pizza

 Prep Time: 10 Minutes   **Cook Time:** 16 Minutes   **Serves:** 2

INGREDIENTS:

- 550g store-bought pizza dough
- 2 tbsp olive oil

Pizza Sauce Ingredients:

- 450ml pizza sauce
- 2 tbsp dried oregano
- 1 tsp garlic-infused oil
- Salt and pepper, to taste
- Toppings:
- 50g mozzarella cheese, sliced
- fresh basil
- 2 tbsp olive oil

INSTRUCTIONS:

- Combine all the ingredients for the pizza sauce in a bowl and set aside.
- Roll the dough on a flat surface and lightly grease it with the oil spray.

- Place the dough in the baking tin or basket of the air fryer and set the temperature to 400 degrees Fahrenheit (204 degrees Celsius) for 10 minutes.
- Once half-baked, remove the pizza and spread the sauce evenly over it.
- Add the basil and mozzarella cheese as toppings.
- Place the pizza back in the air fryer and set the temperature to 400 degrees Fahrenheit (204 degrees Celsius) for 6 minutes.
- Serve once the cheese has melted.

 NUTRITION INFORMATION:

Servings:	2	
Per serving:		
Calories:	848	
Fat:	58.4g	(75% of daily value)
Saturated Fat:	25.4g	(127% of daily value)
Cholesterol:	103mg	(34% of daily value)
Sodium:	2076mg	(90% of daily value)
Carbohydrates:	37.8g	(14% of daily value)
Fiber:	6.1g	(22% of daily value)
Sugars:	7.4g	
Protein:	49.8g	

10 | **Dessert**

173. Air Fryer Toasted Marshmallow Fluff Waffles

 Prep: 16 Minutes | **Cook Time:** 8 Minutes | **Serves:** 2

INGREDIENTS:

- 227 g large marshmallows
- 2 fluffy Belgian style waffles
- 120 ml maple syrup

INSTRUCTIONS:

- Begin by lightly spraying the air fryer basket with non-stick spray to prevent sticking.
- Pack the marshmallows tightly together and place them upright in the air fryer.
- Set the temperature to 350°F (176°C) and cook for 8 minutes.
- Meanwhile, cook the Belgian style waffles according to package instructions.
- Once the marshmallows are done, use a blunt-edged knife or offset spatula to scoop them onto the top of each waffle.
- Drizzle with maple syrup and add additional toppings such as chocolate chips, if desired.

NUTRITION FACTS:

Servings: 2

Per serving:

Calories:	681	
Total Fat:	4.3 g	(5%)
Saturated Fat:	0.7 g	(3%)
Cholesterol:	5 mg	(2%)
Sodium:	346 mg	(15%)
Total Carbohydrates:	159 g	(58%)
Dietary Fiber:	1 g	(3%)
Total Sugars:	101.8 g	
Protein:	3.4 g	

174. Air Fryer S'mores Dip

 Prep: 15 Minutes | **Cook Time:** 6 Minutes | **Serves:** 2

INGREDIENTS:

- 200 g chocolate chips
- 227 g marshmallows
- 8 graham crackers

INSTRUCTIONS:

- Fill the bottom of a 7-inch springform pan or any dish suitable for the air fryer with half of the chocolate chips.
- Add a layer of marshmallows on top of the chocolate chips.
- Cover the marshmallows with the remaining chocolate chips.
- Cook in the air fryer at 350°F (176°C) for 6 minutes, until the chocolate is soft and the marshmallows are light golden-brown.
- Carefully remove from the air fryer and serve with graham crackers or any other preferred dipping items.

NUTRITION FACTS:

Servings: 2

Per serving:

Calories: 960

Total Fat:	30.8 g	(40%)
Saturated Fat:	18.4 g	(92%)
Cholesterol:	19 mg	(6%)
Sodium:	473 mg	(21%)
Total Carbohydrates:	160 g	(58%)
Dietary Fiber:	4.5 g	(16%)
Total Sugars:	100.4 g	
Protein:	11 g	

175. Air Fryer Fruit Pudding

 Prep:
20 Minutes **Cook Time:**
25 Minutes   **Makes:**
3 Servings

INGREDIENTS

- For topping:
- 85g of flour
- 55g sugar
- 1 egg
- 2 tablespoons of milk (30ml)
- 55g of soft butter
- 1/2 tablespoon of baking powder (7.5g)
- For filling:
- 225g of canned or fresh sliced fruit

DIRECTIONS

- Preheat the air fryer to 350 degrees F or 176 degrees C.
- Mix the ingredients for topping in a bowl.
- well for three minutes until the mixture is creamy and soft.
- Pour the filling ingredient into a baking dish, add the topping mixture over the fruit and smoothen the top.
- Bake in a preheated air fryer at 160°C for 25-30 minutes, until golden brown.

NUTRITION FACTS

Servings:	2	
Amount per serving		
Calories	492	
% Daily Value*		
Total Fat	19g	24%
Saturated Fat	4.3g	22%
Cholesterol	83mg	28%
Sodium	189mg	8%
Total Carbohydrate	69.8g	25%
Dietary Fiber	3.1g	11%
Total Sugars	32.3g	
Protein	15.7g	

176. Air Fryer, Easy Peach Cobbler

 Prep:
20 Minutes   **Cook Time:**
10 Minutes   **Makes:**
3 Servings

INGREDIENTS

- 600g of peach pie filling
- 30g of flour
- 225g of sugar
- Cobbler Topping:
- 225g of flour
- 30g of sugar
- 1 teaspoon of baking powder (5g)
- 1 teaspoon of ground cinnamon (2g)
- 1 egg
- 60ml of milk

DIRECTIONS

- Start by mixing peaches, flour, and sugar.
- Pay attention and be sure that all of the peaches are coated.
- Then spray an air fryer safe pan with olive oil, and spread the bottom layer into the pan.
- Then in another bowl, mix the cobbler, the flour, sugar, baking powder, ground cinnamon, egg, and milk.
- Drop the cobbler over the bottom layer.
- Then place the pan in the air fryer basket or the air fryer . Set the temperature to 350 degrees F or 176 degrees C, for about ten minutes.
- Remove once golden on top.
- Set aside to cool before serving it.

NUTRITION FACTS

Servings:	4	
Amount per serving		
Calories	519	
% Daily Value*		
Total Fat	4.4g	6%
Saturated Fat	1g	5%
Cholesterol	43mg	14%
Sodium	101mg	4%
Total Carbohydrate	107.3g	39%
Dietary Fiber	5.2g	19%
Total Sugars	88.6g	
Protein	17.2g	

177. Chocolate Oatmeal Cookies

 Prep: 20 Minutes | **Cook Time:** 12 Minutes | **Makes:** 3 Servings

INGREDIENTS

- 225g quick-cooking oatmeal
- 150g plain flour
- 50g cocoa powder
- 200g packet of instant chocolate pudding mix
- 2 teaspoons of baking soda
- 225g unsalted butter, softened
- 200g brown sugar
- 3 large eggs
- 2 teaspoons of vanilla extract
- 225g chocolate chips
- Non-stick cooking spray

DIRECTIONS

- Preheat the air fryer to 350ºF (176ºC) for a few minutes.
- Coat the air fryer sheet with non-stick cooking spray.
- Mix the flour, baking soda, oats, cocoa powder, pudding mix, and salt in a mixing bowl.
- In another dish, whisk together the cream butter and brown sugar using a hand mixer.
- Add the vanilla essence and the eggs.
- Combine the oats and the other ingredients in a large mixing basin.
- Add the chocolate chips and stir until all of the ingredients are well mixed.
- Drop dough onto a baking sheet in the shape of a cookie scoop.
- BAKE for 12 minutes in the air fryer, or until it becomes light brown.
- Cool using a wire rack, and serve.

NUTRITION FACTS

Servings:	4	
Amount per serving		
Calories	1203	
% Daily Value*		
Total Fat	38.2g	49%
Saturated Fat	22.5g	113%
Cholesterol	153mg	51%
Sodium	910mg	40%
Total Carbohydrate	192g	70%
Dietary Fiber	15.5g	55%
Total Sugars	80g	
Protein	29.2g	

178. Air Fryer Beignets

 Prep: 15 Minutes | **Cook Time:** 7 Minutes | **Makes:** 3-4 Servings

INGREDIENTS

- 225g Self-Rising Flour
- 200g plain Greek Yogurt
- 45g caster sugar
- 2 teaspoons of vanilla extract
- 45g melted unsalted butter
- Canola oil spray

DIRECTIONS

- Mix the yogurt, sugar, and vanilla.
- Add in the flour until it forms a dough.
- Place the dough on a floured work surface.
- Several times fold the dough in 1/2.
- Preheat the air fryer to 350ºF (176ºC).
- Spray the air fryer tray/basket with canola spray.
- Brush the tops of the dough with melted butter.
- Place butter side down on the tray or basket.
- Air fry for about 6-7 minutes until they are golden brown.

NUTRITION FACTS

Servings:	3	
Amount per serving		
Calories	709	
% Daily Value*		
Total Fat	16.3g	21%
Saturated Fat	3.4g	17%
Cholesterol	0mg	0%
Sodium	407mg	18%
Total Carbohydrate	57.3g	21%
Dietary Fiber	6.6g	23%
Total Sugars	44.7g	
Protein	80g	

179. Black Forest Hand Pies

 Prep: 18 Minutes | **Cook Time:** 18 Minutes | **Makes:** 2 Servings

INGREDIENTS

- 200g dark chocolate chips
- 90g hot fudge sauce
- 75g chopped dried cherries
- 1 sheet of puff pastry

- 2 egg whites, beaten
- 45g sugar
- 1 teaspoon cinnamon

DIRECTIONS

- In a mixing bowl, mix the chocolate chips, hot fudge sauce, and the chopped dried cherries.
- The puff pastry should now be laid out on a floured board.
- Preheat the air fryer to 176°C.
- The bowl mixture should be put in the center of the puff pastry, which should be sliced into 6 pieces.
- To create triangles, fold the puff pastry in half.
- Brush the egg whites on the sides of the triangles and push the dough corners together tightly.
- Sprinkle cinnamon and sugar streusel on top.
- In the air fryer basket, bake for 18 minutes at 160°C, or until it becomes golden brown.
- Set aside to cool before serving.

NUTRITION FACTS

Servings: 2

Amount per serving

Calories:	2178 kJ	
Total Fat	27.3g	35%
Saturated Fat	17.9g	89%
Cholesterol	60mg	20%
Sodium	344mg	15%
Total Carbohydrate	66.2g	24%
Dietary Fiber	4.9g	17%
Total Sugars	46.1g	
Protein	8.3g	

180. Air Fryer Oreos

 Prep: 10 Minutes   **Cook Time:** 7 Minutes   **Makes:** 3 Servings

INGREDIENTS

- 2 cans of Crescents Dough
- 10 Oreo cookies
- 30g to 90g powdered sugar

DIRECTIONS

- Spread the dough evenly over the Oreos, ensuring there are no air bubbles and that the cookies are fully covered.
- Place the wrapped Oreos on the air fryer rack or basket, and cook for 4 minutes on the lowest rack setting at 176°C.

- After 3-4 minutes, flip the Oreos once the tops have become a light golden-brown color.
- Before serving, sprinkle the Oreos with powdered sugar after they've been cooked.

NUTRITION FACTS

Servings: 2

Amount per serving

Calories:	1519 kJ	
Total Fat	14.5g	19%
Saturated Fat	3.8g	19%
Cholesterol	0mg	0%
Sodium	542mg	24%
Total Carbohydrate	55.8g	20%
Dietary Fiber	2.5g	9%
Total Sugars	27.2g	
Protein	4.7g	

181. Chocolate Chip Cookie

 Prep: 20 minutes   **Cook Time:** 10 minutes   **Serves:** 3

INGREDIENTS:

- 75g butter, softened
- 200g brown sugar
- 2 egg yolks
- 175g plain flour
- 75g ground white chocolate
- 1.5 tsp baking soda
- 2 tsp vanilla extract
- 180g chocolate chips

INSTRUCTIONS:

- In a mixing bowl, cream together the butter and brown sugar until light and fluffy.
- Beat in the egg yolks.
- Stir in the flour, ground white chocolate, baking soda, and vanilla extract until well combined.
- Fold in the chocolate chips.
- Line a small baking pan with parchment paper.
- Spread the batter evenly into the pan, leaving a 2.5 cm border around the edges.
- Preheat the air fryer to 176°C.
- Bake the cookie in the air fryer for 10 minutes, or until lightly golden brown.
- Remove from the air fryer and allow to cool on a wire rack before serving.

NUTRITION INFORMATION (PER SERVING):

Calories:	814
Fat:	41.8g
Saturated Fat:	21.6g

Cholesterol:	144mg
Sodium:	731mg
Total Carbohydrates:	112.1g
Dietary Fiber:	6.6g
Total Sugars:	83.2g
Protein:	13.3g

182. Chocolate Peanut Butter Bread Pudding

 Prep: 24 minutes | **Cook Time:** 15 minutes | **Serves:** 3

INGREDIENTS:

- 2 large eggs
- 2 egg yolks
- 180ml chocolate milk
- 2 tbsp cocoa powder
- 4 tbsp brown sugar
- 5 tbsp peanut butter
- 3 tsp vanilla extract
- 6 slices firm, cubed white bread
- Oil spray

INSTRUCTIONS:

- In a mixing bowl, whisk together the eggs, egg yolks, chocolate milk, cocoa powder, and brown sugar.
- Spray a baking pan with oil spray.
- Stir in the peanut butter, vanilla extract, and bread cubes.
- Allow the bread to soak in the mixture for a few minutes.
- Preheat the air fryer to 176°C.
- Bake the bread pudding in the air fryer for 15 minutes.
- Serve hot or cooled, as desired.

NUTRITION INFORMATION (PER SERVING):

Calories:	613
Fat:	33.5g
Saturated Fat:	9.7g
Cholesterol:	385mg
Sodium:	477mg
Total Carbohydrates:	56.7g
Dietary Fiber:	5.4g
Total Sugars:	31.9g
Protein:	24.9

183. Lime Cheesecake

 Prep: 24 Minutes | **Cook Time:** 25 Minutes | **Serves:** 3

INGREDIENTS

- 10 Digestive biscuits
- 150g melted Butter
- 450g soft Cheese
- 225g caster Sugar
- 5 large Eggs
- 45ml Honey
- 2 Limes
- 90g Greek Yogurt
- 1 tsp Vanilla extract

INSTRUCTIONS

- Preheat the air fryer to 176°C (350°F).
- Dust the sides of a springform tin with flour to prevent sticking.
- Crush the digestive biscuits into crumbs using your hands or a rolling pin.
- In a mixing bowl, combine the melted butter and biscuit crumbs and press into the bottom of the springform tin.
- In another mixing bowl, beat the sugar and cheese together with a hand mixer until the mixture thickens and the sugar is evenly distributed.
- In a separate dish, whisk the eggs, honey, and vanilla extract together.
- In a third mixing bowl, combine the limes, zest, and juice. Add the Greek yogurt and mix well with a fork.
- Spoon the cheese mixture into the air fryer and cook for 10 minutes at 160°C (320°F).
- Spoon the lime mixture over the cheese mixture and smooth with a spatula.
- Increase the temperature to 190°C (375°F) and cook for another 15 minutes.
- Let the cheesecake cool for at least 6 hours before serving.

NUTRITION INFORMATION (PER SERVING)

Servings:	4	
Calories:	1120	
Total Fat:	61.5g	(79%)
Saturated Fat:	34.7g	(174%)
Cholesterol:	372mg	(124%)
Sodium:	770mg	(33%)
Total Carbohydrate:	97g	(35%)
Dietary Fiber:	0.5g	(2%)
Total Sugars:	84.6g	
Protein:	46.5g	

184. Ginger Cranberry Scones

 Prep: 24 Minutes | **Cook Time:** 15 Minutes | **Makes:** 3-4 Servings

INGREDIENTS

- To make the Ginger Cranberry Scones the following ingredients should be got
- 140g of plain flour
- 25g of dark brown sugar
- 1 tsp of baking powder
- 1 tsp of ground cinnamon
- 2 tsp of freshly grated nutmeg
- 2 tsp of ground cloves
- 2 tsp of salt
- A pinch of ginger powder
- 200g of dried cranberries
- 100g unsalted butter, frozen, grated on a box grater
- 160ml heavy cream, plus more for glazing
- 2 tsp of vegetable oil
- 2 large eggs
- 2 tsp of vanilla extract
- 200g of sour cream
- Demerara sugar, for sprinkling

DIRECTIONS

- After the ingredients have been gathered, follow these steps to achieve the desired result
- First, you have to preheat the air fryer to 350 degrees F or 176 degrees C.
- Mix the flour, sugar, baking soda, baking powder, nutmeg, cinnamon, salt, cloves, ginger, and cranberries in a large basin.
- Add the grated butter after that.
- In a separate bowl, whisk together heavy cream, egg, vanilla, and sour cream.
- In a mixing dish, combine the wet and dry ingredients.
- Form the dough into a 8cm thick circle.
- Cut the dough into 8 wedges.
- Using vegetable oil and Demerara sugar, toss the top of the wedge.
- Put it in an air fryer basket and cook for 15 minutes.
- Rotate the scones, halfway through.
- Serve and enjoy.

NUTRITION FACTS

Servings: 4

Amount per serving

Calories 1140

% Daily Value*		
Total Fat	78.2g	100%
Saturated Fat	46.6g	233%
Cholesterol	278mg	93%
Sodium	1560mg	68%
Total Carbohydrate	90.7g	33%
Dietary Fiber	5.5g	20%
Total Sugars	9.1g	
Protein	17.5g	

185. Coconut Meringues

 Prep: 10 Minutes | **Cook Time:** 3 Hours 30 Minutes | **Makes:** 1 Serving

INGREDIENTS

- 1/4 teaspoon cream of tartar
- Salt, to taste
- 4 egg whites
- 100g granulated sugar
- 1/2 teaspoon coconut extract

DIRECTIONS

- Using an electric whisk, beat the egg whites to a smooth consistency.
- Add the salt, coconut extract, sugar, and cream of tartar to the mixture.
- Beat with the electric whisk until stiff peaks form, then transfer to a piping bag.
- Line the air fryer basket with parchment paper.
- Pipe the mixture onto the lined basket.
- Cook at 80 degrees C for 3-4 hours.
- Once cooked, let cool before serving.

NUTRITION FACTS

Servings: 2

Amount per serving

Calories 226

% Daily Value*		
Total Fat	0.1g	0%
Saturated Fat	0g	0%
Cholesterol	0mg	0%
Sodium	144mg	6%
Total Carbohydrate	50.8g	18%
Dietary Fiber	0g	0%
Total Sugars	50.6g	
Protein	7.2g	

186. Air Fryer Banana Cream Pie

 Prep: 25 Minutes | **Cook Time:** 12 Minutes | **Makes:** 2 Servings

INGREDIENTS

- 1 packet mini graham cracker crusts
- 1 packet pudding mix
- more Milk , for pudding
- 1 container whipped cream
- 1 banana

DIRECTIONS

- Remove the crust and place them in the air fryer.
- Set the temperature to 176 degrees Celsius for 2 minutes.
- Let the pie shell cool down.
- Prepare pudding with milk in a saucepan.
- Pour the prepared pudding into the pie shell and let it cool in the refrigerator.
- Top the pie shell with whipped cream and sliced bananas.
- Serve and enjoy!

 NUTRITION FACTS

Servings:	2	
Amount per serving		
Calories	965	
% Daily Value*		
Total Fat	55.6g	71%
Saturated Fat	22.3g	111%
Cholesterol	93mg	31%
Sodium	787mg	34%
Total Carbohydrate	108.7g	40%
Dietary Fiber	3.6g	13%
Total Sugars	66.6g	
Protein	11.8g	

187. Nutella Banana Bread Pudding Cups

 Prep: 25 Minutes | **Cook Time:** 10 Minutes | **Makes:** 2 Servings

INGREDIENTS

- 125 ml almond milk
- A few drops of vanilla extract
- 2-4 slices of cubed bread
- 2 eggs
- 80 g Nutella
- 1 banana

DIRECTIONS

- Take a mixing bowl and add the milk and a few drops of vanilla extract.
- Then add the cubed bread to the bowl.
- In another bowl, whisk together the eggs and Nutella.

- Pour the egg mixture over the bread in the mixing bowl.
- Spray muffin cups with oil spray.
- Pour the prepared mixture into the cups.
- Bake in an air fryer at 176 degrees Celsius for 10 minutes.
- Once baked, serve the bread pudding and enjoy.

 NUTRITION FACTS

Servings:	2	
Amount per serving		
Calories	306	
% Daily Value*		
Total Fat	18.2g	23%
Saturated Fat	15g	75%
Cholesterol	41mg	14%
Sodium	198mg	9%
Total Carbohydrate	33.4g	12%
Dietary Fiber	3.8g	14%
Total Sugars	13.7g	
Protein	5.6g	

188. Air Fryer Blueberry Apple Crumble

 Prep: 25 Minutes | **Cook Time:** 15 Minutes | **Makes:** 3-4 Servings

INGREDIENTS

- Blueberry Apple Filling
- 450g fresh blueberries
- 120g apple sauce
- 2 tsp granulated sugar
- 2 tsp vanilla extract
- 1 tsp lemon zest
- Crumble Topping
- 50g all-purpose flour
- 20g quick oats
- 40g granulated sugar
- 40g unsalted butter
- 1 pinch salt

DIRECTIONS

- Clean the blueberries and place them in the pan then add apple sauce with lemon zest to it.
- Then combine the sugar and vanilla and top it over the blueberries.
- Combine the dry ingredients for the streusel until the mixture gets crumbly.
- Place the crumbles over the blueberry mixture and bake at 176 degrees C for 15 minutes.
- Cook until the streusel becomes golden brown. Serve and enjoy.

NUTRITION FACTS

Servings: 3

Amount per serving

Calories   226

% Daily Value*

Total Fat	11.9g	15%
Saturated Fat	7.4g	37%
Cholesterol	31mg	10%
Sodium	133mg	6%
Total Carbohydrate	28.2g	10%
Dietary Fiber	0.8g	3%
Total Sugars	12.1g	
Protein	2.5g	

Printed in Great Britain
by Amazon

21958324R00057